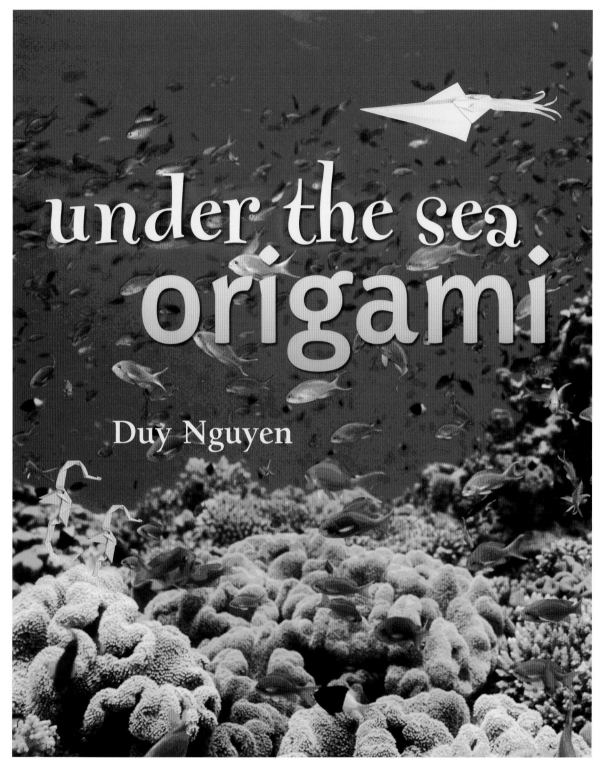

under the sea
origami

Duy Nguyen

Sterling Publishing Co., Inc.
New York

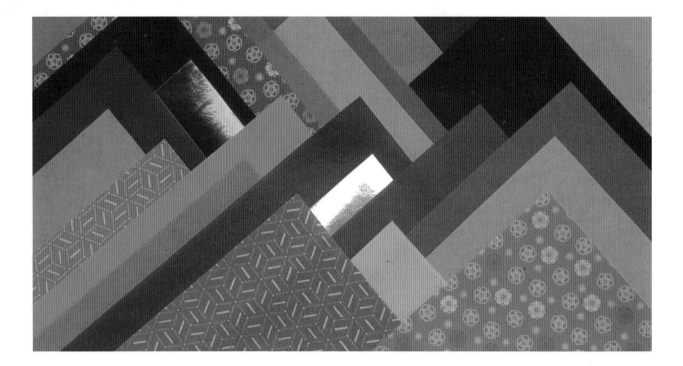

Design by Judy Morgan
Edited by Claire Bazinet

Library of Congress Cataloging-in-Publication Data
Nguyen, Duy, 1960-
  Under the Sea Origami / Duy Nguyen.
    p. cm.
  Includes index.
  ISBN 1-4027-1541-2
  1. Origami. 2. Fishes in art. I. Title.
TT870.N48823 2004
736'.982--dc22

               2004003341

10 9 8 7 6 5 4 3 2 1

Published by Sterling Publishing Co., Inc.
387 Park Avenue South, New York, NY 10016
© 2004 by Duy Nguyen
Distributed in Canada by Sterling Publishing
℅ Canadian Manda Group, One Atlantic Avenue, Suite 105
Toronto, Ontario, Canada M6K 3E7
Distributed in Great Britain and Europe by Chris Lloyd at Orca Book
Services, Stanley House, Fleets Lane, Poole BH15 3AJ, England
Distributed in Australia by Capricorn Link (Australia) Pty. Ltd.
P.O. Box 704, Windsor, NSW 2756, Australia
Printed in China

Sterling ISBN 1-4027-1541-2

Contents

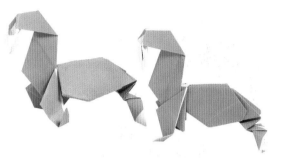

Basic Folds 6

kite fold ◆ valley fold ◆ mountain fold ◆ inside reverse fold ◆ outside reverse fold ◆ pleat fold ◆ pleat fold reverse ◆ squash fold I ◆ squash fold II ◆ inside crimp fold ◆ outside crimp fold

Base Folds 10

base fold I ◆ base fold II ◆ base fold III ◆ base fold IV

Creative Projects 16

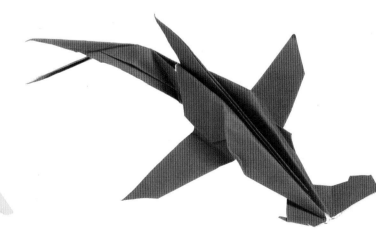

Preface

A word of encouragement. When I first began learning origami, I struggled with even the simplest folds. I would look back at the instructions at the beginning of the book again and again, reviewing the basic folds. I also looked ahead, at the diagram showing the next step of whatever project I was folding, to see how it *should* look, to be certain I was following the instructions correctly. Looking ahead at the "next step," the result of a fold, is incidentally a very good way for a beginner to learn origami.

You will easily pick up this and other learning techniques as you follow the step-by-step directions and fold the simple origami forms specially designed for this book. Soon you'll find yourself with an under-the-sea origami menagerie perfectly suited for display in a large—but waterless—bedroom aquarium. Or, you can simply enjoy making dozens of these colorful sea creatures and present them to family members and special friends.

Duy Nguyen

Basic Instructions

Paper: Paper used in traditional origami is thin, keeps a crease well, and folds flat. Packets of specially designed sheets, about 6 and 8 inches square (15 and 21 cm), can be found in various colors. Many of the the simpler projects in this book, however, call for a longer, rectangular-shaped paper, but this shouldn't be a problem. Colored papers, for use in crafts, are widely available. You can also use plain white paper, solid-color paper, or even wrapping paper. Be aware, though, that some papers stretch slightly in length or width, while others tear easily.

You might also color or print off your own larger sheets and cut to size. Use markers to add coloring to white paper and sea-appropriate finishing touches. (While regular white paper may be too heavy for traditional origami, it is fine for crafting these simpler creatures. Their fewer folds also make them perfect for learning to fold and enjoy the wonderful art of origami.)

Glue: Use an easy-flowing but not loose paper glue. Use it sparingly; don't soak the paper. A flat toothpick makes a good applicator. Be sure to allow the glued form time to dry. Avoid stick glue, which can become overly dry and crease or damage your figure.

Technique: Fold with care. Position the paper, especially at corners, precisely and line edges up before creasing. Once you are sure of the fold, use a fingernail to make a clean, flat crease.

For more complex folds, create "construction lines." Fold and unfold, using simple mountain and valley folds, to pre-crease. This creates guidelines, and the finished fold is more likely to match the one shown in the book. Folds that look different, because the angles are slightly different, can throw you off. Don't get discouraged with your first efforts. In time, what your mind can create, your fingers can fashion.

Symbols & Lines

Fold lines	valley	Fold then unfold	← →
	mountain		
Cut line		Pleat fold (repeated folding)	
Turn over or rotate		Crease line	

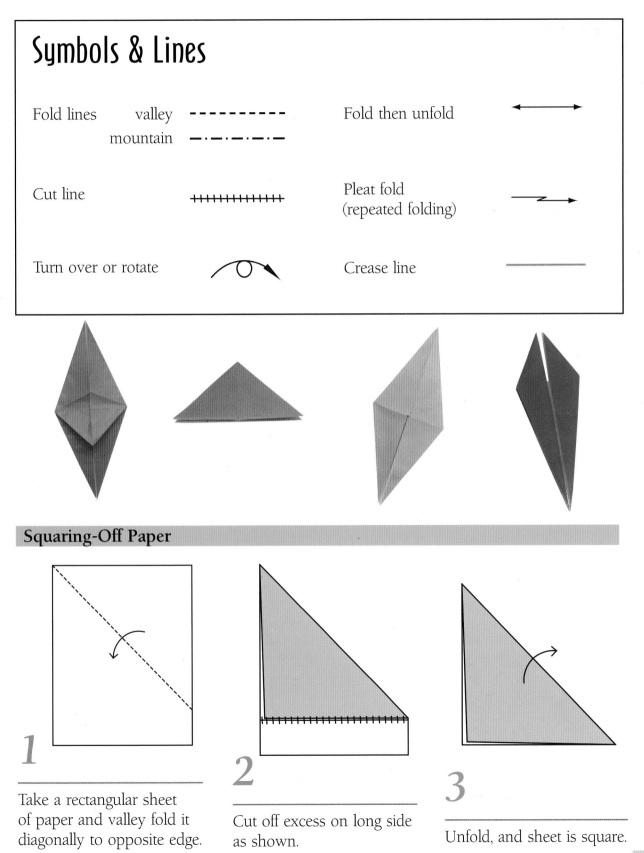

Squaring-Off Paper

1
Take a rectangular sheet of paper and valley fold it diagonally to opposite edge.

2
Cut off excess on long side as shown.

3
Unfold, and sheet is square.

Basic Folds

Kite Fold

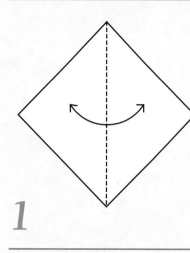

1
Fold and unfold a square diagonally, making a center crease.

2
Fold both sides in to the center crease.

3
This is a kite form.

Valley Fold   - - - - - - - - - - - - - - - -

1
Here, using the kite, fold form toward you (forward), making a "valley."

2
This fold forward is a valley fold.

Mountain Fold   - · - · - · - · - · - · - · -

1
Here, using the kite, fold form away from you (backwards), making a "mountain."

2
This fold backwards is a mountain fold.

Inside Reverse Fold

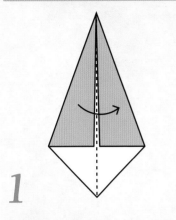

1

Starting here with a kite, valley fold kite closed.

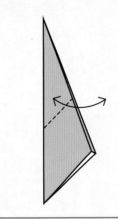

2

Valley fold as marked to crease, then unfold.

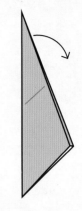

3

Pull tip in direction of arrow.

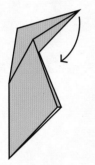

4

Appearance before completion.

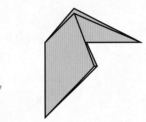

5

You've made an inside reverse fold.

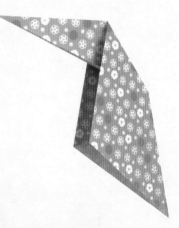

Outside Reverse Fold

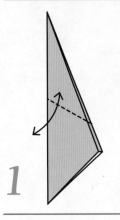

1

Using closed kite, valley fold, unfold.

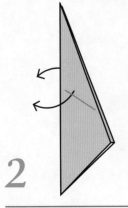

2

Fold inside out, as shown by arrows.

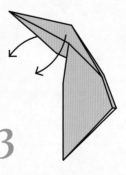

3

Appearance before completion.

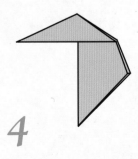

4

You've made an outside reverse fold.

Basic Folds

7

Pleat Fold

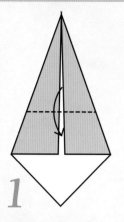

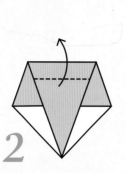

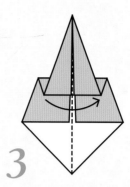

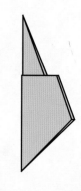

1 Here, using the kite, valley fold.

2 Valley fold back again.

3 This is a pleat. Valley fold in half.

4 You've made a pleat fold.

Pleat Fold Reverse

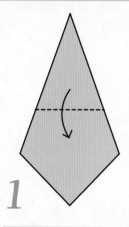

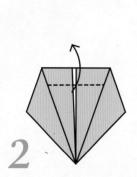

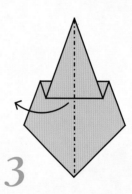

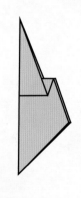

1 Here, using the kite form backwards, valley fold.

2 Valley fold back again for pleat.

3 Mountain fold form in half.

4 This is a pleat fold reverse.

Squash Fold I

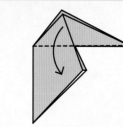

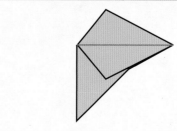

1 Using inside reverse, valley fold one side.

2 This is a squash fold I.

Squash Fold II

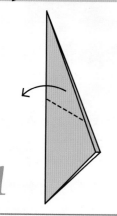

1

Using closed kite form, valley fold.

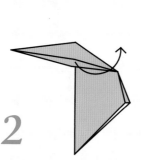

2

Open in direction of the arrow.

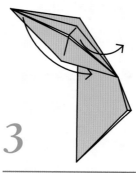

3

Appearance before completion.

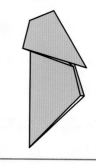

4

You've made a squash fold II.

Inside Crimp Fold

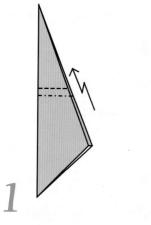

1

Here, using closed kite form, pleat fold.

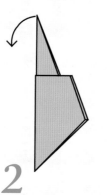

2

Pull tip in direction of the arrow.

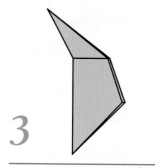

3

This is an inside crimp fold.

Outside Crimp Fold

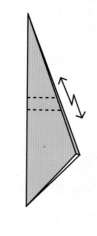

1

Here, using closed kite form, pleat fold and unfold.

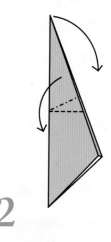

2

Fold mountain and valley as shown, both sides.

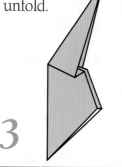

3

This is an outside crimp fold.

Basic Folds

9

Base Folds

Base folds are basic forms that do not in themselves produce origami, but serve as a basis, or jumping-off point, for a number of creative origami figures, some quite complex. As when beginning other crafts, learning to fold these base folds is not the most exciting part of origami. They are, however, easy to do, and will help you with your technique. They also quickly become rote, so much so that you can do many using different-colored papers while you are watching television or your mind is elsewhere. With completed base folds handy, if you want to quickly work up a form or are suddenly inspired with an idea for an original, unique figure, you can select an appropriate base fold and swiftly bring a new creation to life.

Base Fold I

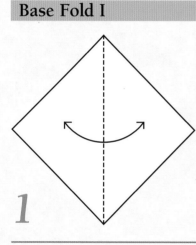

1

Fold and unfold in direction of arrow.

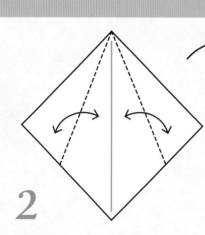

2

Fold both sides in to center crease, then unfold. Rotate.

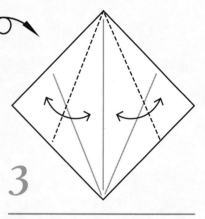

3

Fold both sides in to center crease, then unfold.

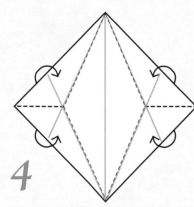

4

Pinch corners of square together and fold inward.

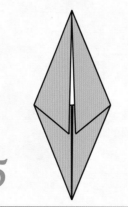

5

Completed Base Fold I.

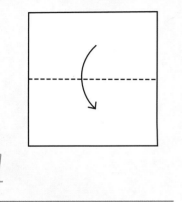

1

Valley fold.

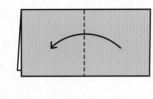

2

Valley fold.

3

Squash fold.

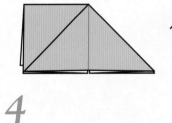

4

Turn over to other side.

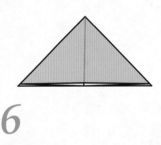

5

Squash fold.

6

Completed Base Fold II.

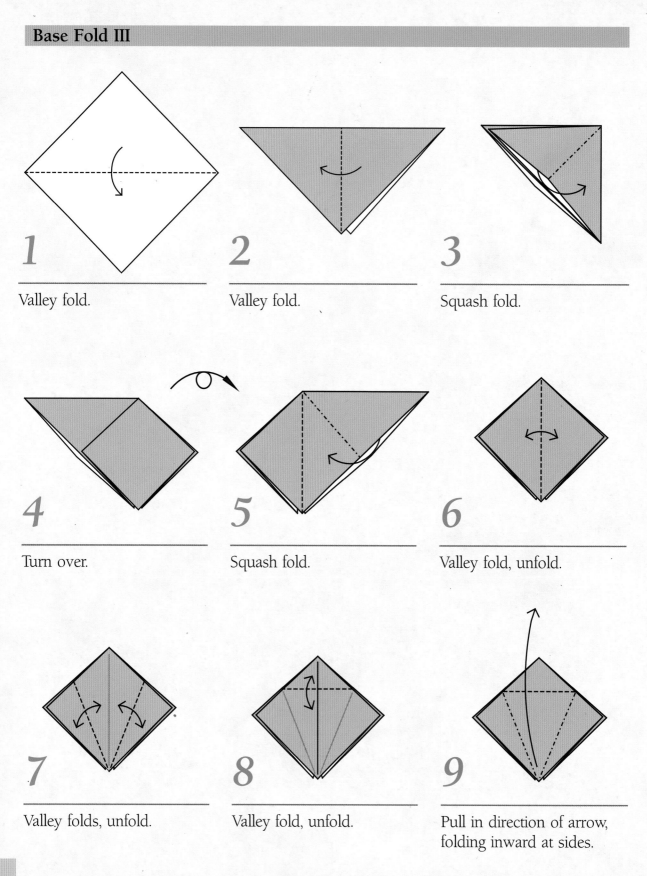

1 Valley fold.

2 Valley fold.

3 Squash fold.

4 Turn over.

5 Squash fold.

6 Valley fold, unfold.

7 Valley folds, unfold.

8 Valley fold, unfold.

9 Pull in direction of arrow, folding inward at sides.

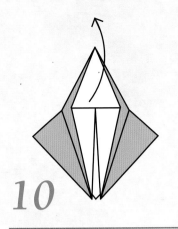

10

Appearance before completion of fold.

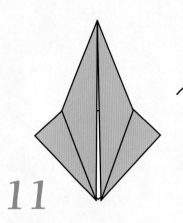

11

Fold completed. Turn over.

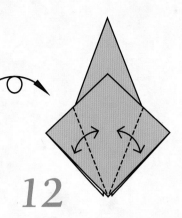

12

Valley folds, unfold.

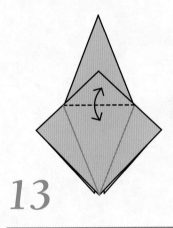

13

Valley fold, unfold.

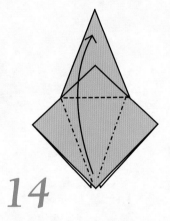

14

Repeat, again pulling in direction of arrow.

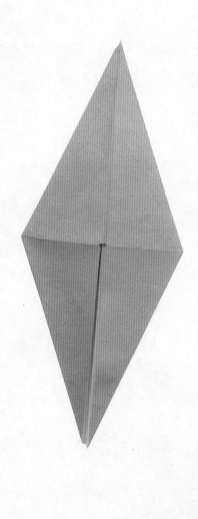

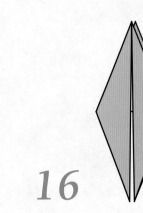

15

Appearance before completion.

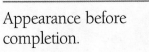

16

Completed Base Fold III.

1

Valley fold rectangular size paper (size variable) in half as shown.

2

Valley fold in direction of arrow.

3

Make cut as shown.

4

Unfold.

5

Unfold.

6

Valley fold in half.

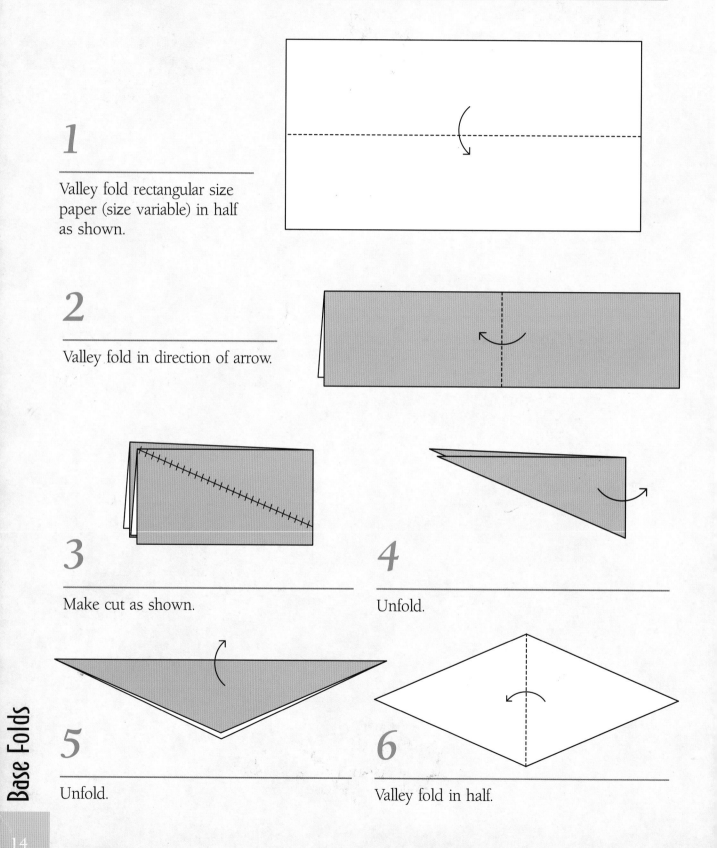

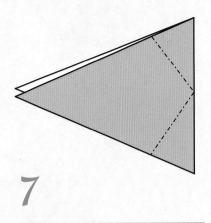

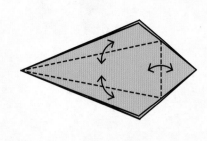

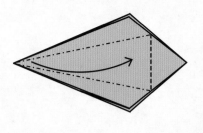

7

Inside reverse folds to inner center crease.

8

Valley fold and unfold to crease.

9

Pull in direction of arrow, and fold.

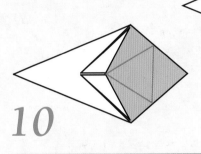

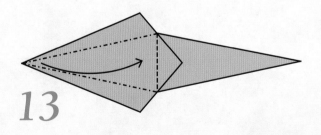

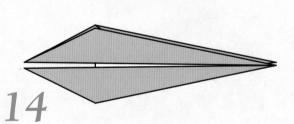

10

Appearance before completion.

11

Turn over.

12

Valley fold then unfold.

13

Again, pull in direction of arrow, and fold.

14

Completed Base Fold IV.

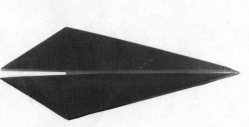

Electric Eel

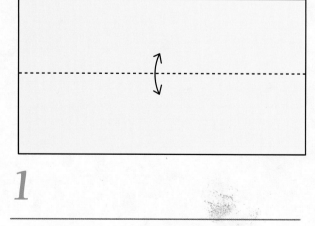

1

Start with a long rectangle (about 4" by 8").
Fold in half and then unfold.

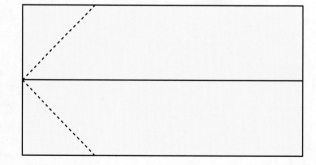

2

Valley folds to center.

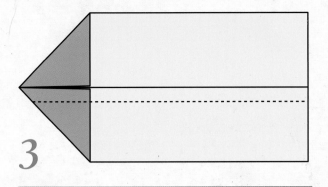

3

Valley fold.

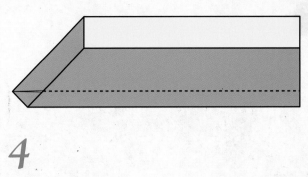

4

Repeat downward.

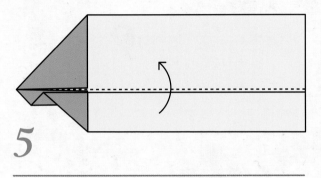

5

Valley fold in half, as shown by arrow.

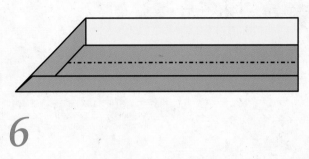

6

Mountain fold. Hide edge inside top layer.

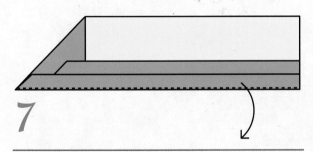

7

Valley fold flap downward.

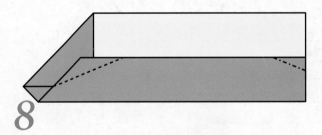

8

Valley fold and mountain fold.

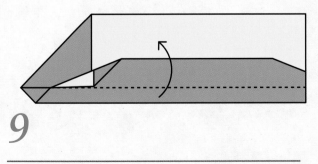

9

Valley fold.

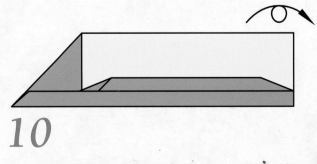
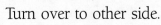

10

Turn over to other side.

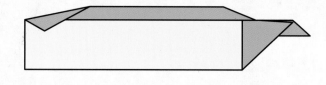

11

Cut and valley fold.

12

Hide behind front layer.

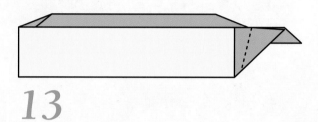

13

Valley fold.

14

Mountain fold.

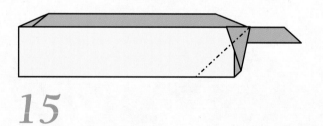

15

Mountain fold.

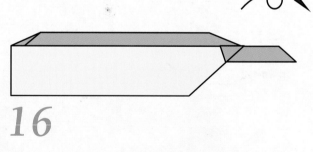

16

Turn over to other side.

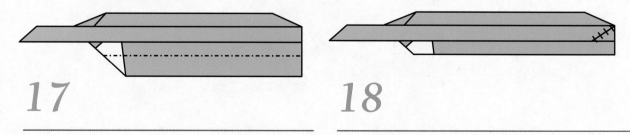

17

Mountain fold.

18

Cut as shown.

19

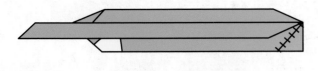

Cut as shown.

20

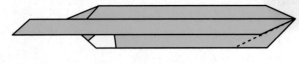

Valley fold.

21

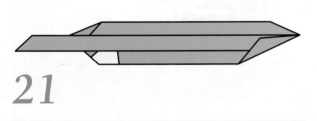

Tuck flap behind front layer.

22

See close-ups for details.

23

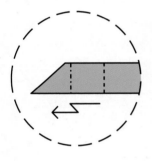

Pleat fold.

24

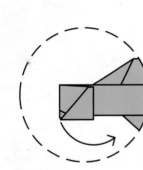

Pull and squash fold.

25

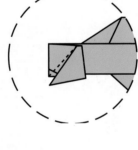

Valley fold both sides.

26

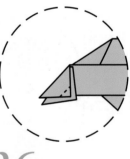

Repeat valley folds. Return to full view.

27

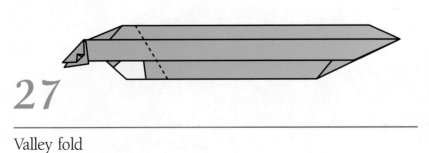

Valley fold

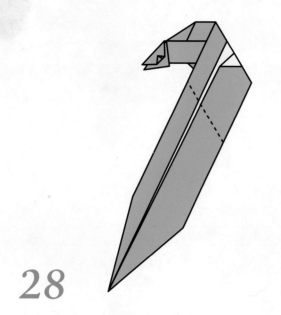

28

Valley fold.

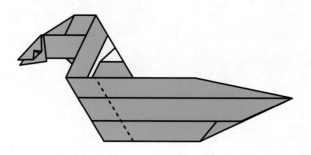

29

Valley fold.

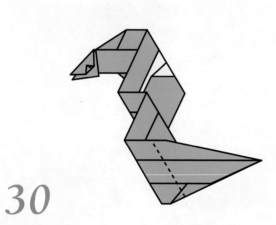

30

Valley fold.

31

Press and pull firmly at the folds to form into curves.

32

Completed Electric Eel.

Dolphin

Part 1

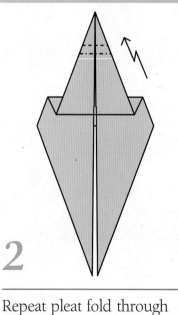

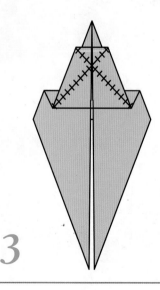

1

Start with Base Fold III.
Pleat fold through all layers.

2

Repeat pleat fold through
layers.

3

Make cuts as shown (to top
layer only).

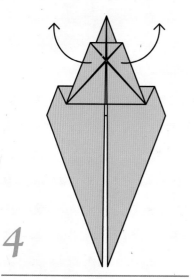

4

Valley folds.

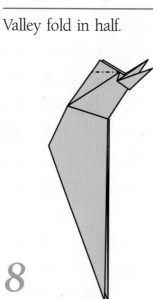

5

Valley fold in half.

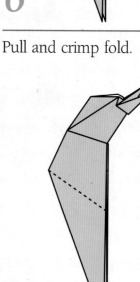

6

Pull and crimp fold.

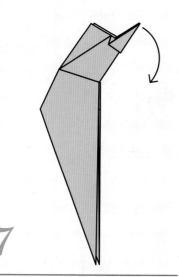

7

Pull and crimp fold.

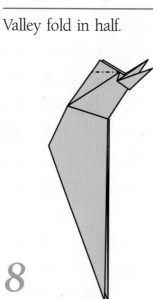

8

Mountain fold.

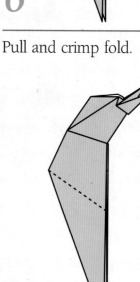

9

Valley folds.

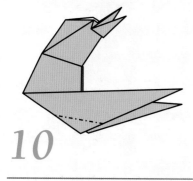

10

Mountain fold both sides.

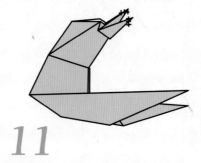

11

Cuts as shown.

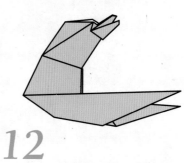

12

Completed part 1 of dolphin.

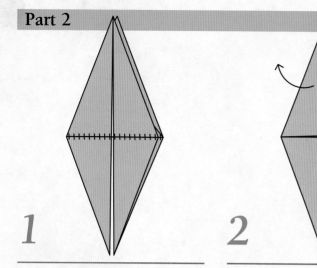

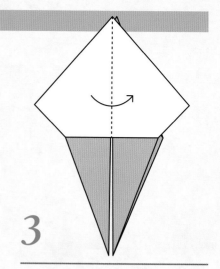

1

Start with Base Fold III.
Cut as shown.

2

Valley folds.

3

Valley fold in half.

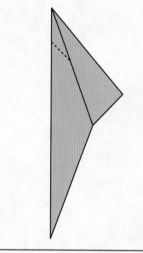

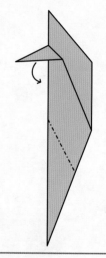

4

Outside reverse fold.

5

Mountain fold.

6

Pull paper outward at top;
mountain fold below.

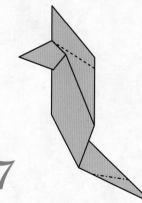

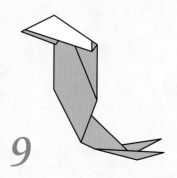

7

Outside reverse at top.
Mountain fold below.

8

Valley fold and glue into
position.

9

Completed part 2
of dolphin.

Dolphin

24

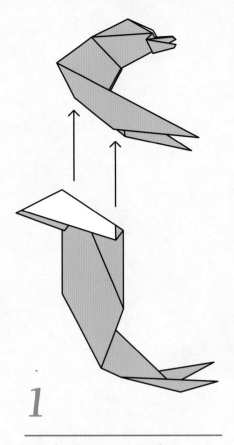

1

Join both parts together as shown.

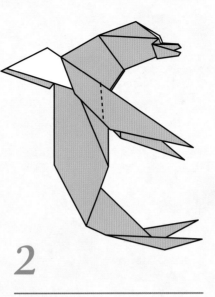

2

Valley fold both sides.

3

Completed Dolphin.

Stingray

Part 1

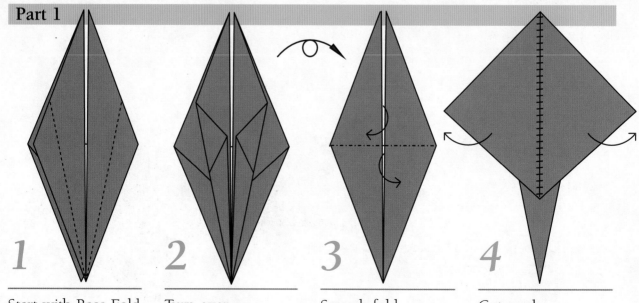

1

Start with Base Fold III. Valley folds.

2

Turn over.

3

Squash fold.

4

Cut as shown. Valley folds.

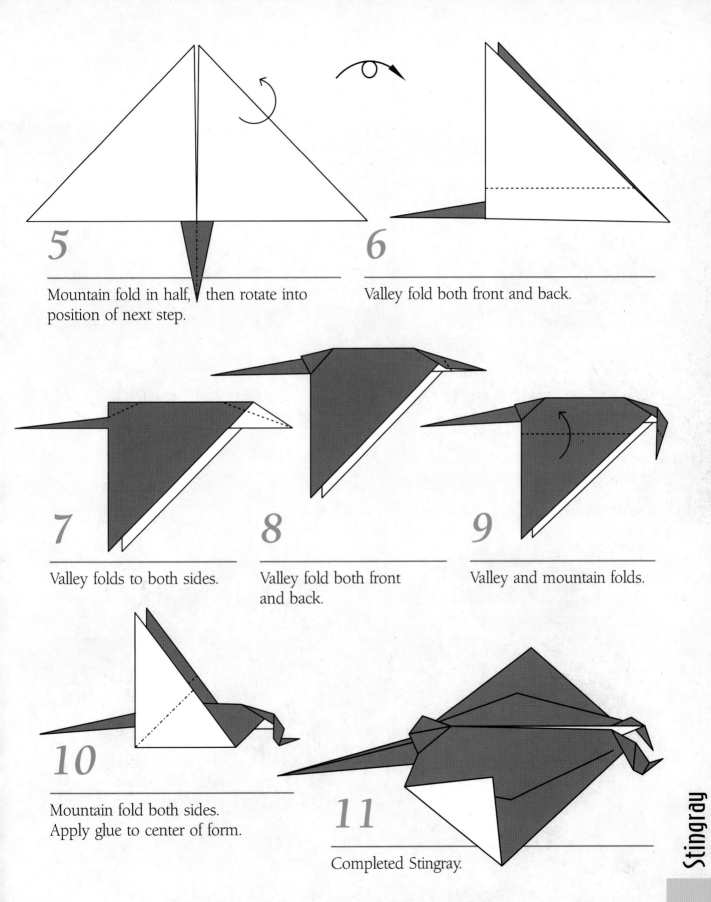

5

Mountain fold in half, then rotate into position of next step.

6

Valley fold both front and back.

7

Valley folds to both sides.

8

Valley fold both front and back.

9

Valley and mountain folds.

10

Mountain fold both sides. Apply glue to center of form.

11

Completed Stingray.

Stingray

Walrus

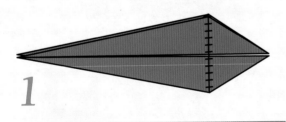

1

Start with Base Fold IV. Make cut as shown.

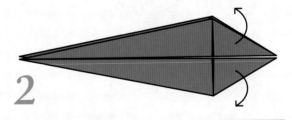

2

Valley fold cut parts.

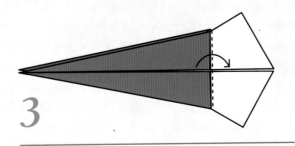

3

Valley fold.

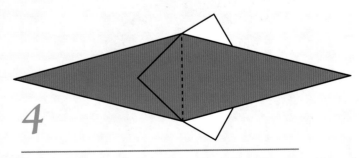

4

Valley fold.

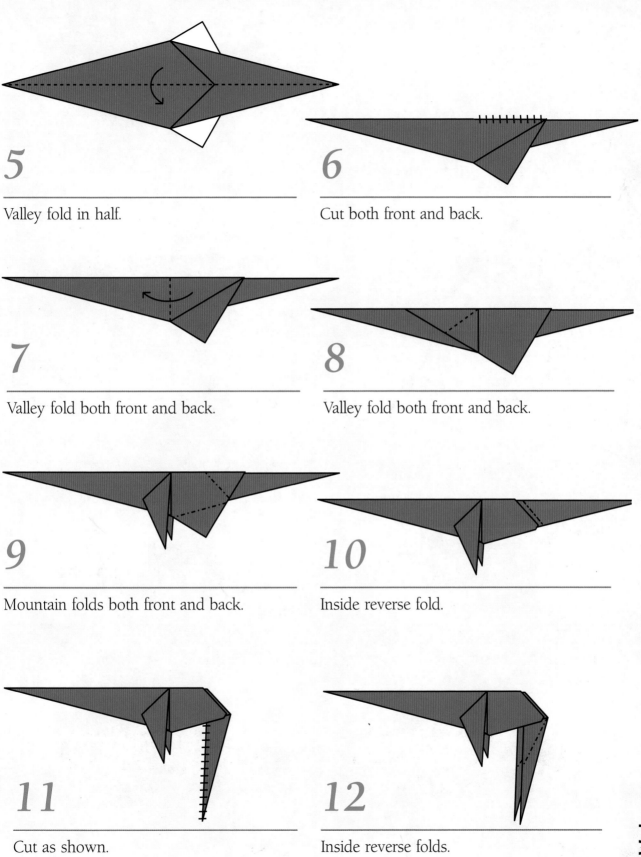

5

Valley fold in half.

6

Cut both front and back.

7

Valley fold both front and back.

8

Valley fold both front and back.

9

Mountain folds both front and back.

10

Inside reverse fold.

11

Cut as shown.

12

Inside reverse folds.

Walrus

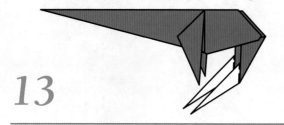

13

Inside reverse folds and squash folds.

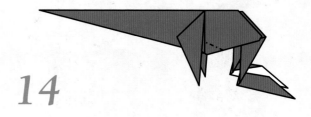

14

Mountain fold both front and back.

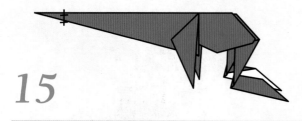

15

Cut top layer as shown.

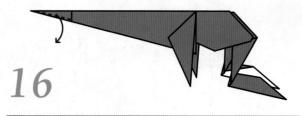

16

Valley fold cut part.

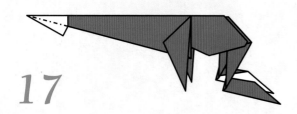

17

Mountain fold both sides.

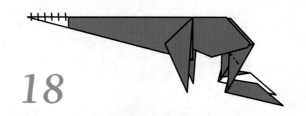

18

Mountain folds front and back. Cut edge as shown.

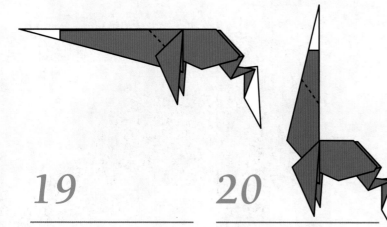

19

Outside reverse fold.

20

Outside reverse fold.

21

See close-ups for detail.

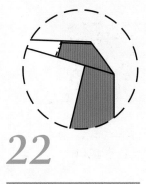

22

Inside reverse fold.

23

Valley folds.

24

Mountain folds.

25

Cuts as shown.

26

Return to full view.

27

Cut as shown, both sides.

28

Valley folds both front and back.

29

Completed Walrus.

Hammerhead Shark

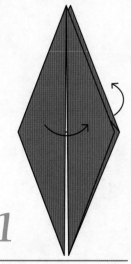

1

Start with Base Fold III. Valley one flap and repeat behind.

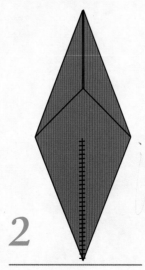

2

Cut as shown front and back.

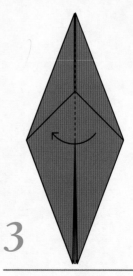

3

Valley fold flap back again. Repeat behind.

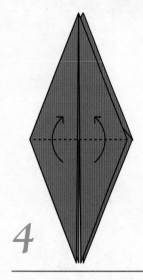

4

Valley folds upward.

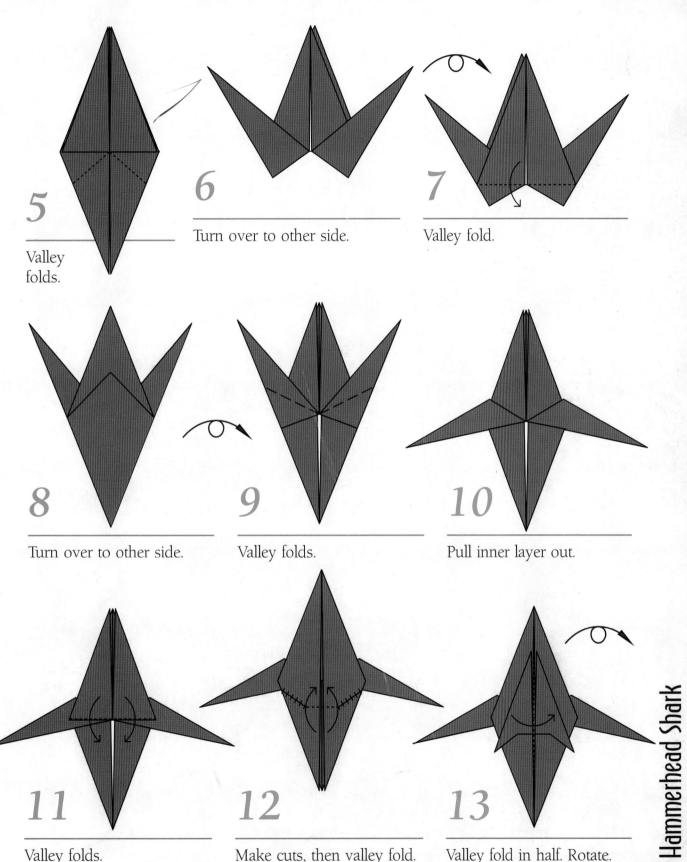

5

Valley folds.

6

Turn over to other side.

7

Valley fold.

8

Turn over to other side.

9

Valley folds.

10

Pull inner layer out.

11

Valley folds.

12

Make cuts, then valley fold.

13

Valley fold in half. Rotate.

Hammerhead Shark

33

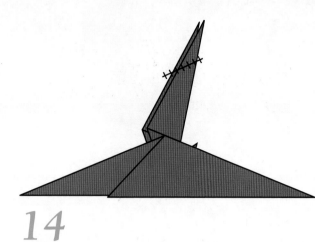

14

Cuts as shown.

15

Valley folds both front and back.

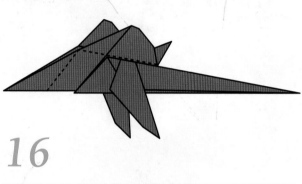

16

Outside reverse fold. Valley fold.

17

Cut edge as shown.

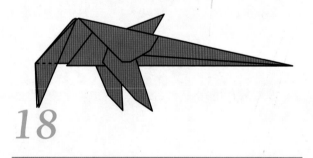

18

Valley fold both front and back.

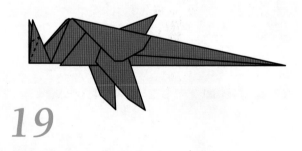

19

Squash fold both front and back.

20

Valley fold sides outward, to balance.

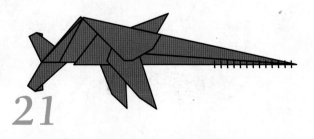

21

Make cut as shown.

22

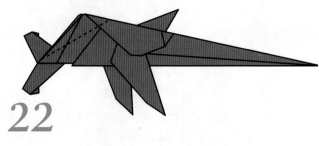

Valley folds both front and back.

23

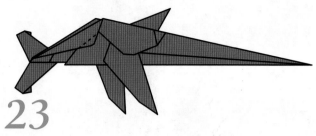

Valley folds both front and back.

24

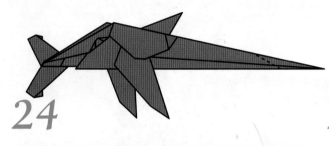

Valley folds both front and back.

25

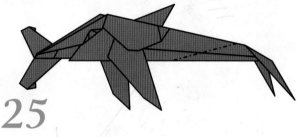

Mountain fold.

26

Valley fold both sides, position to balance.

27

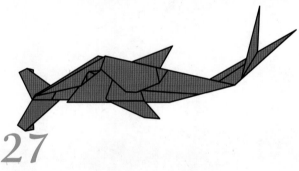

Adjust tail, fins, and head to balance.

28

Completed Hammerhead Shark.

Horseshoe Crab

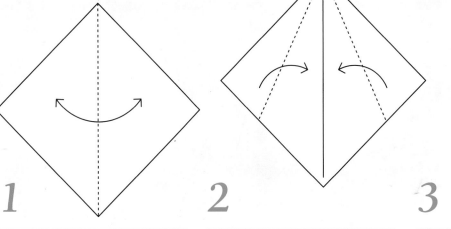

1

Start with square. Valley fold and unfold.

2

Fold both sides inward.

3

Pleat fold.

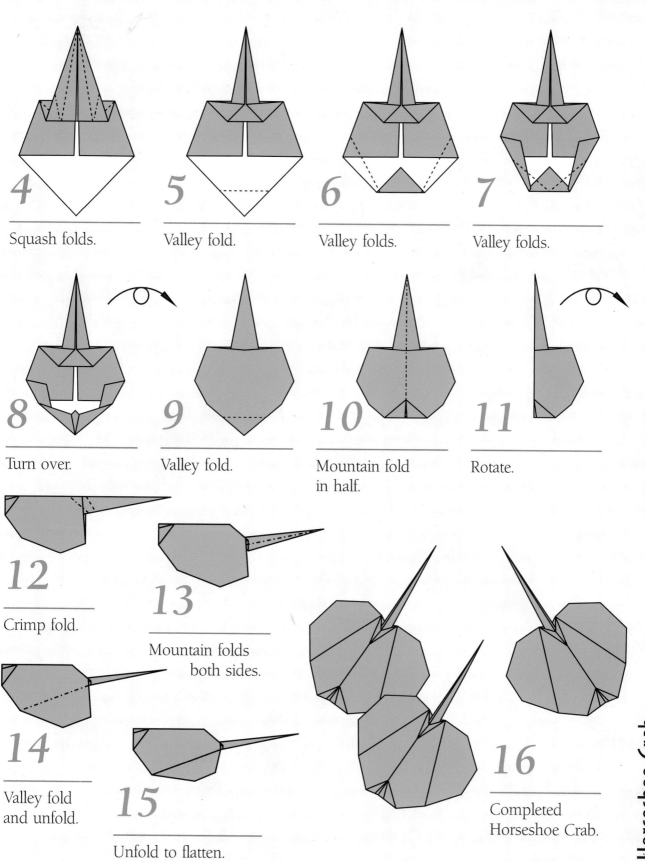

4 Squash folds.

5 Valley fold.

6 Valley folds.

7 Valley folds.

8 Turn over.

9 Valley fold.

10 Mountain fold in half.

11 Rotate.

12 Crimp fold.

13 Mountain folds both sides.

14 Valley fold and unfold.

15 Unfold to flatten.

16 Completed Horseshoe Crab.

Angelfish

1

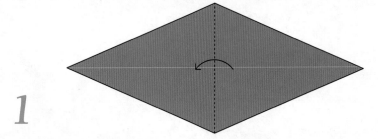

Start with Step 5 (diamond shape) of Base Fold IV.
Valley fold in half.

2

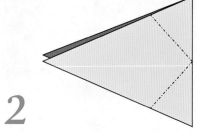

Inside reverse folds.

3

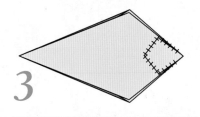

Cuts to front layer only.

4

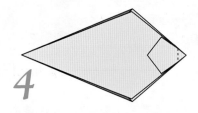

Valley fold cut parts.

5

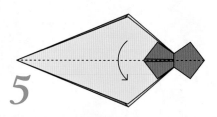

Valley fold front and back.

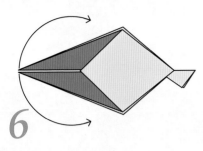

6

Inside reverse folds.

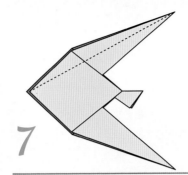

7

Valley fold front and back.

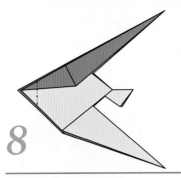

8

Mountain fold layer inward.

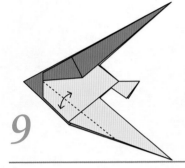

9

Valley fold layer and unfold.

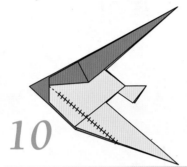

10

Cut along crease. Valley fold.

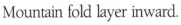
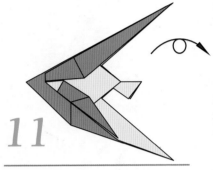

11

Turn over to other side.

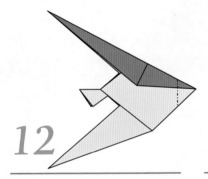

12

Mountain fold.

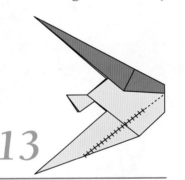

13

Cut as shown, valley fold.

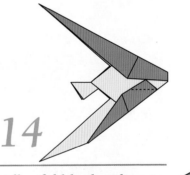

14

Valley fold both side fins outward.

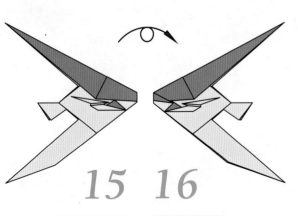

15   16

Turn over.   Add color.

17

Completed Angelfish.

Angelfish

Lionfish

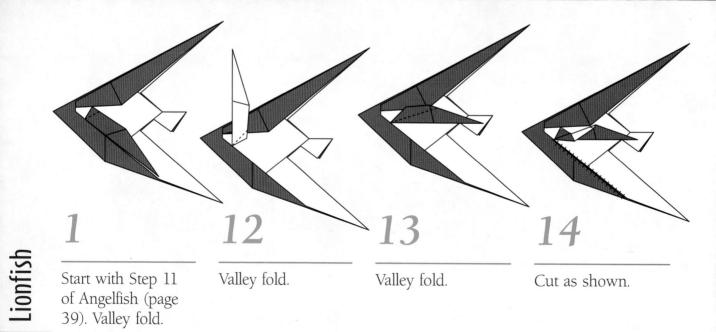

1
Start with Step 11 of Angelfish (page 39). Valley fold.

12
Valley fold.

13
Valley fold.

14
Cut as shown.

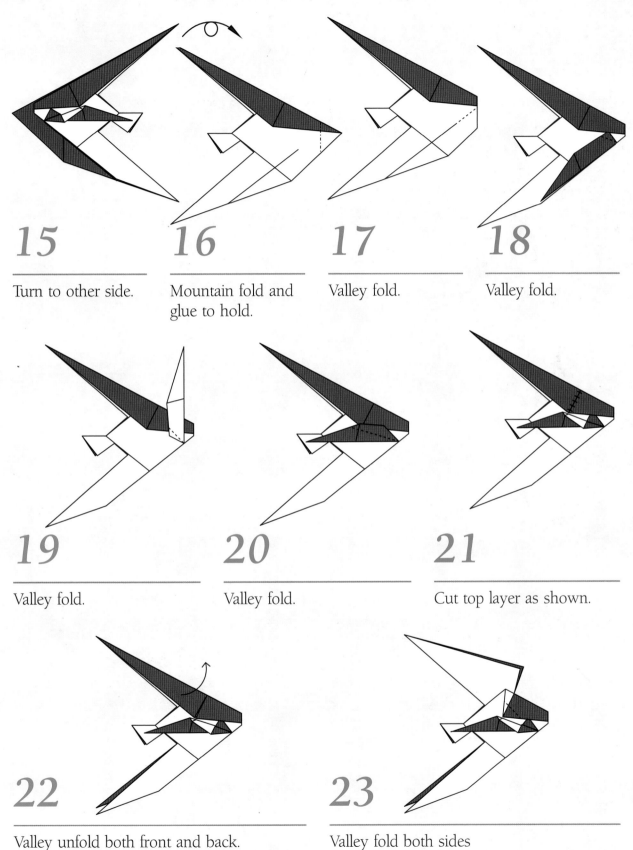

15
Turn to other side.

16
Mountain fold and glue to hold.

17
Valley fold.

18
Valley fold.

19
Valley fold.

20
Valley fold.

21
Cut top layer as shown.

22
Valley unfold both front and back.

23
Valley fold both sides

Lionfish

41

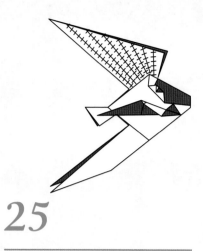

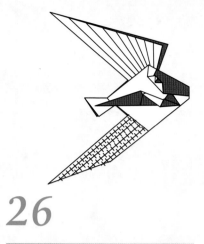

24

Valley folds front and back.

25

Cut as shown to both sides.

26

Repeat cuts, to lower section.

27

Valley fold front and back.

28

Repeat.

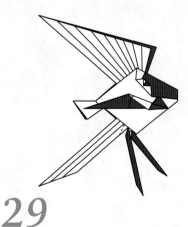

29

Repeat.

30

Repeat.

31

Repeat.

32

Valley fold side fins loosely to extend.

33

Loosely valley fold at top also, both sides.
Add any color and patterning wanted.

34

Completed Lionfish.

Seahorse

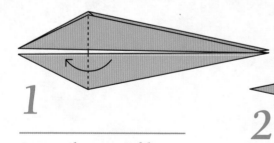

1

Start with Base Fold IV.
Valley fold.

2

Turn over to other side.

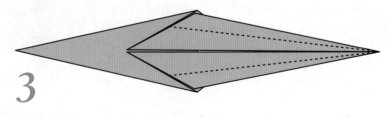

3

Valley fold both sides.

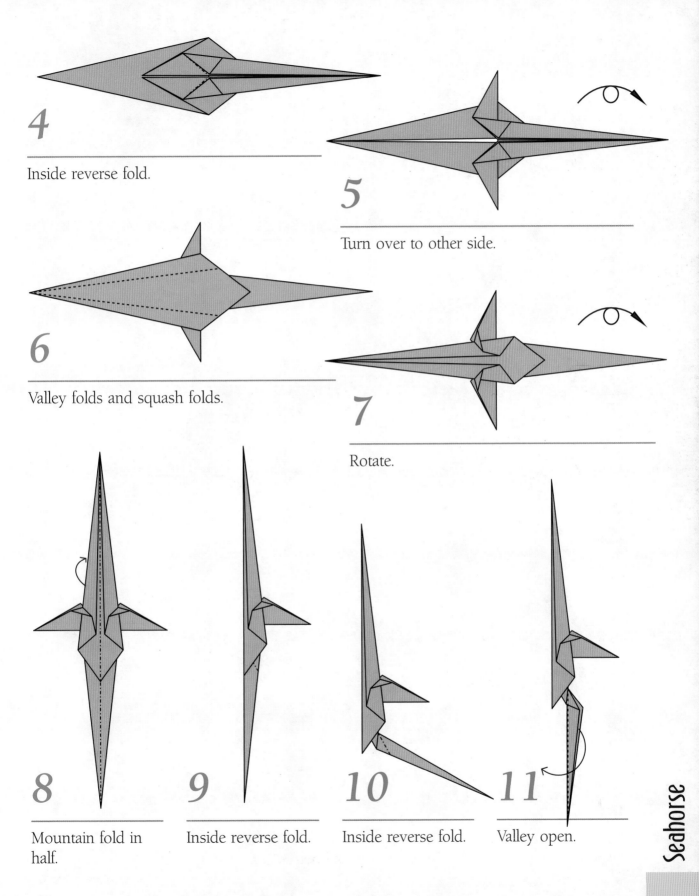

4

Inside reverse fold.

5

Turn over to other side.

6

Valley folds and squash folds.

7

Rotate.

8

Mountain fold in half.

9

Inside reverse fold.

10

Inside reverse fold.

11

Valley open.

Seahorse

45

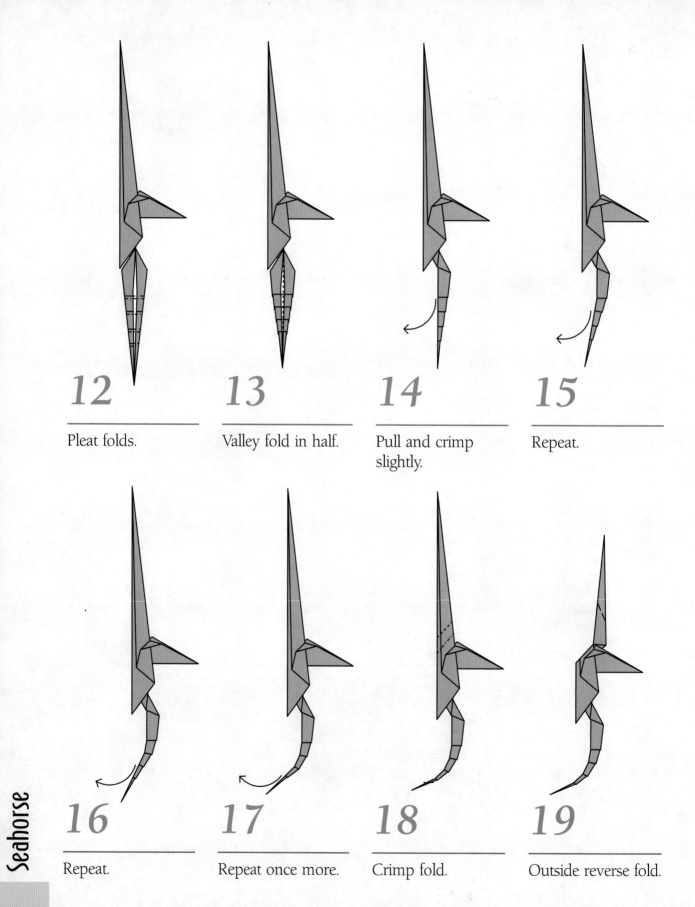

12
Pleat folds.

13
Valley fold in half.

14
Pull and crimp slightly.

15
Repeat.

16
Repeat.

17
Repeat once more.

18
Crimp fold.

19
Outside reverse fold.

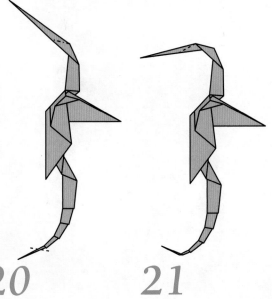

20

Inside and outside reverse folds.

21

Valley fold both sides.

22

Pleat fold and crimp into position.

23

Outside reverse folds.

24

Inside reverse fold.

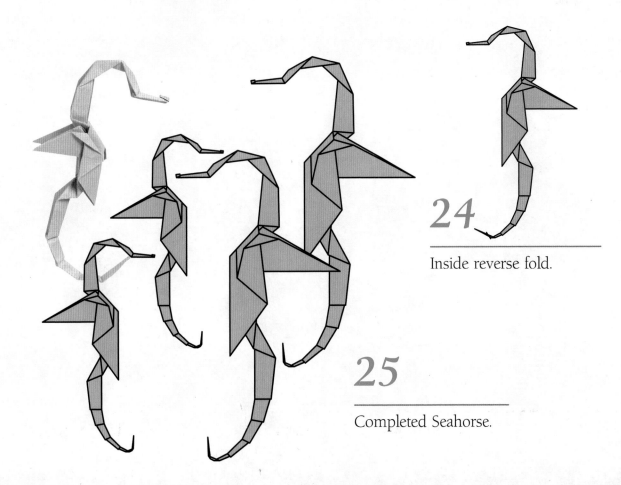

25

Completed Seahorse.

Flying Fish

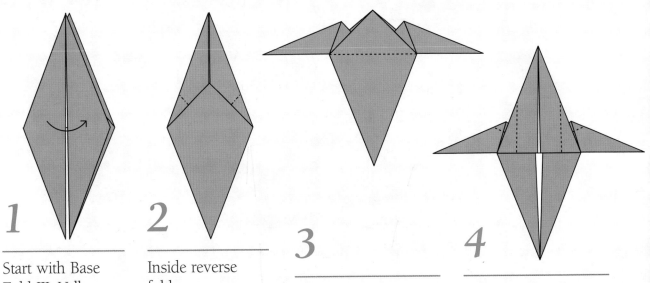

1

Start with Base Fold III. Valley folds.

2

Inside reverse folds.

3

Valley fold.

4

Valley folds. Squash at same time.

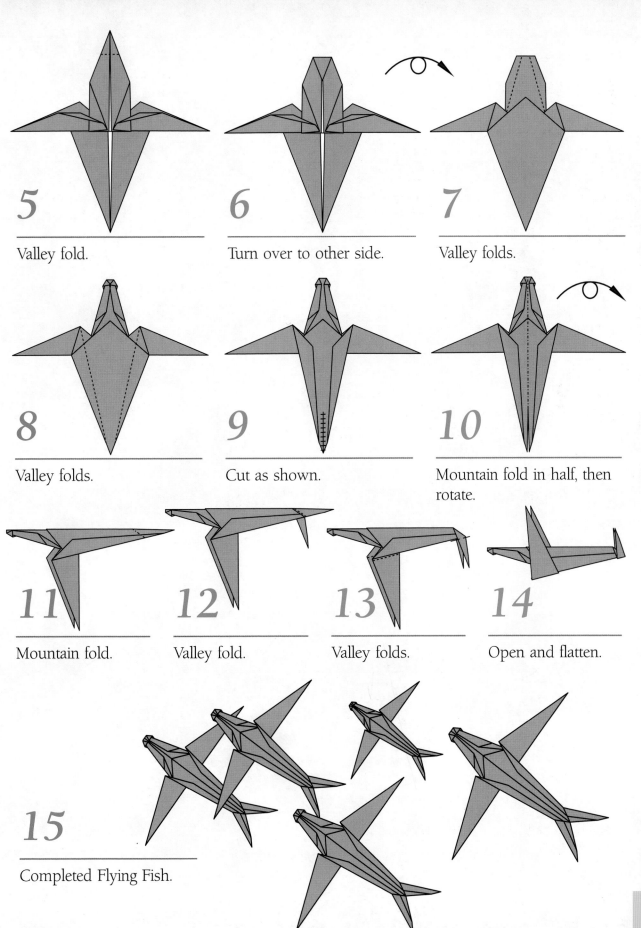

5

Valley fold.

6

Turn over to other side.

7

Valley folds.

8

Valley folds.

9

Cut as shown.

10

Mountain fold in half, then rotate.

11

Mountain fold.

12

Valley fold.

13

Valley folds.

14

Open and flatten.

15

Completed Flying Fish.

Flying Fish

Barracuda

1

Start with rectangular paper (about 3.5" by 11") and valley fold.

2

Make cuts as shown.

3

Valley fold both sides.

4

Inside reverse fold.

5

Outside reverse fold.

6

Inside reverse fold.

7

Valley fold both sides.

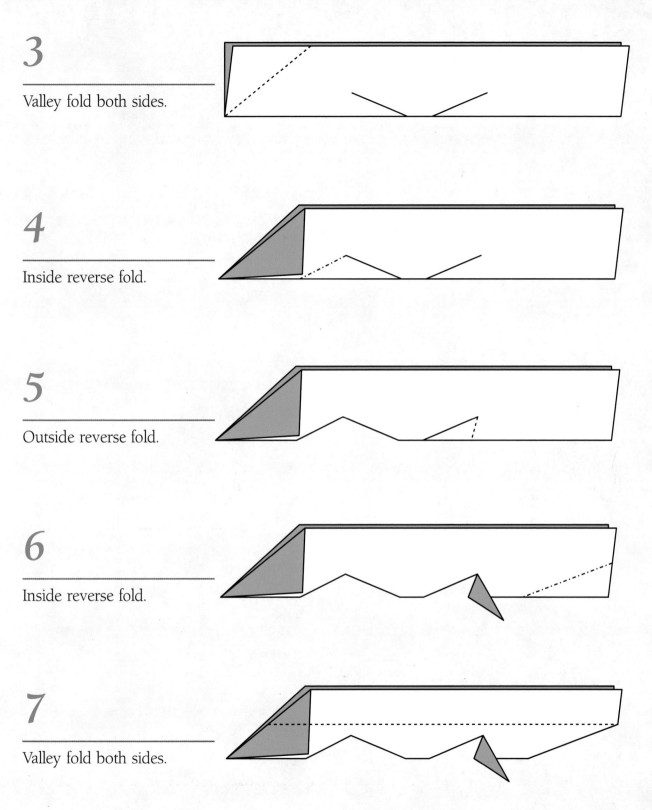

8

Cut as shown.

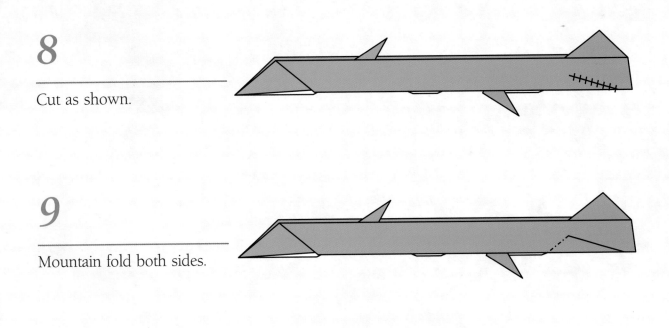

9

Mountain fold both sides.

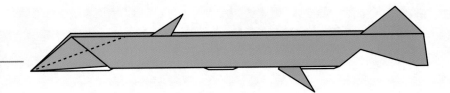

10

Valley fold both sides.

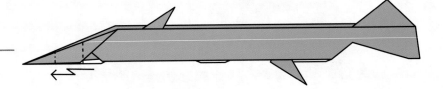

11

Pleat fold.

12

Valley fold both sides.

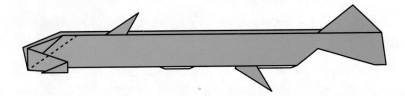

13

Valley fold both sides.

14

Make cuts to both sides.

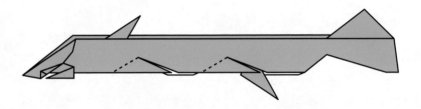

15

Valley folds both sides.
Add coloring if wanted.

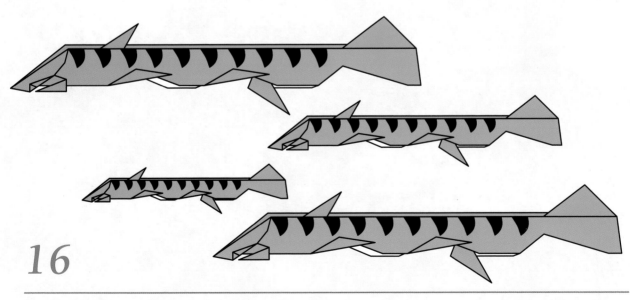

16

Completed Barracuda.

Baby Tiger Shark

1

Cut rectangular paper (about 4" by 11") into diamond shape (see page 14). Turn over.

2

Continue folding into Base Fold IV.

3

Valley fold.

4

Fold in half.

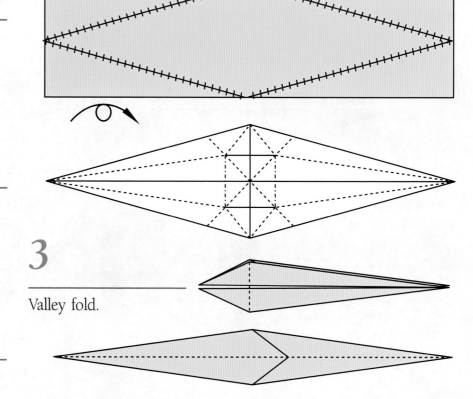

5

Valley fold both sides.

6

Inside reverse fold.

7

Valley fold both front and back.

8

Valley fold both sides.

9

Inside reverse fold.

10

Valley fold both front and back.

11

Valley fold and unfold to crease.

12

Pull and press creased lines to form a natural body curve.

13

Completed Baby Tiger Shark.

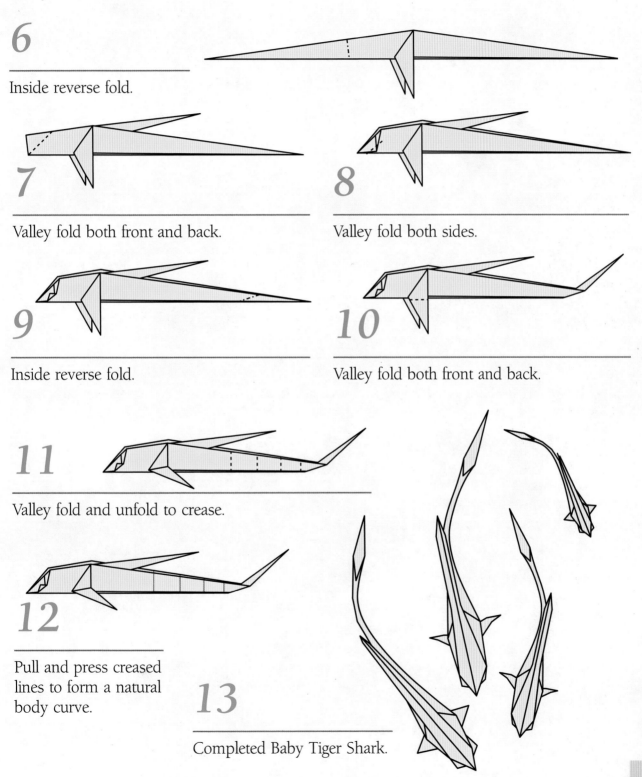

Baby Tiger Shark

55

Humpback Whale

Part 1

1

Cut rectangular paper (about 4" by 11") into diamond shape (see page 14). Turn over.

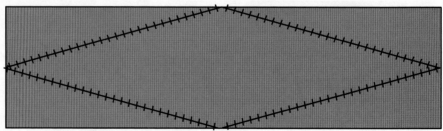

2

Continue folding into Base Fold IV

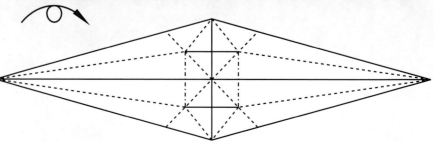

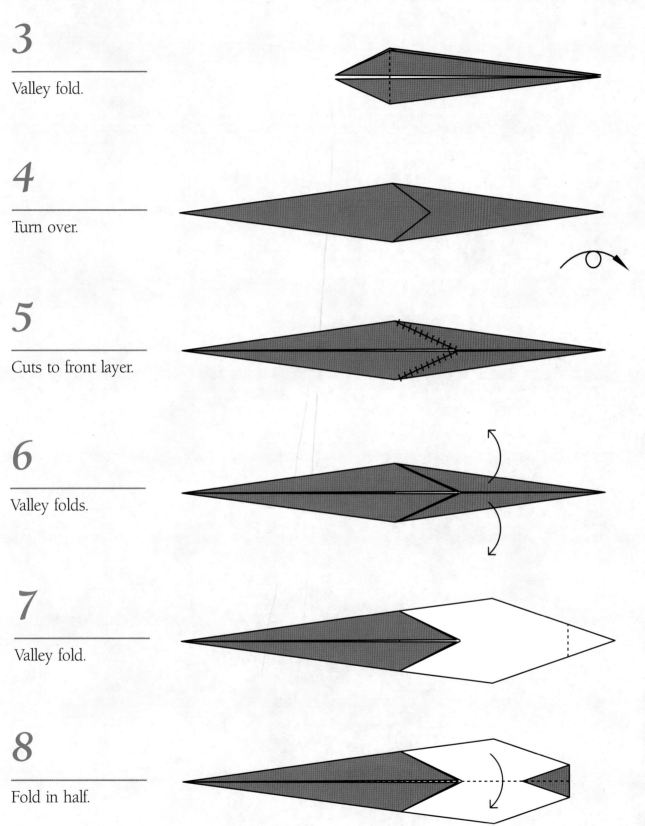

3

Valley fold.

4

Turn over.

5

Cuts to front layer.

6

Valley folds.

7

Valley fold.

8

Fold in half.

Humpback Whale

9

Cut as shown.

10

Valley fold.

11

Mountain fold.

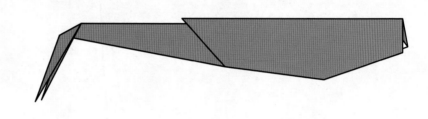

12

Completed part 1 of whale.

Part 2

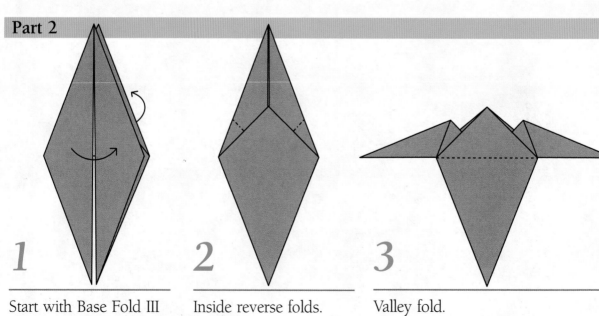

1

Start with Base Fold III from 8.5" square. Valley over, front and back.

2

Inside reverse folds.

3

Valley fold.

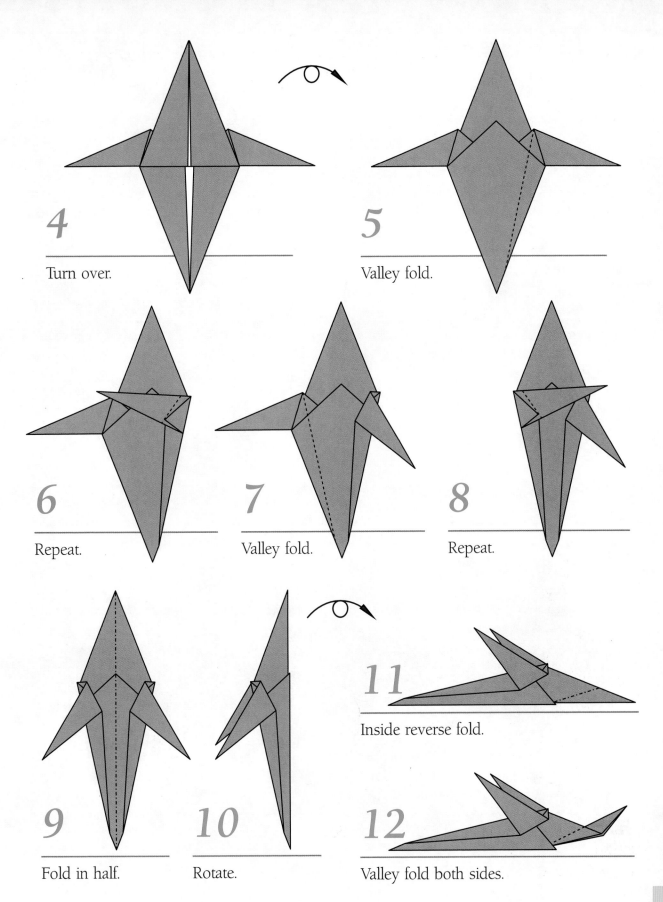

4

Turn over.

5

Valley fold.

6

Repeat.

7

Valley fold.

8

Repeat.

9

Fold in half.

10

Rotate.

11

Inside reverse fold.

12

Valley fold both sides.

Humpback Whale

13

Cut as shown. Valley fold upward both front and back.

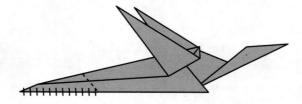

14

Pull down and outward as shown.

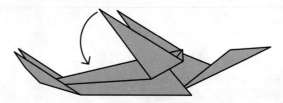

15

Make cuts as shown.

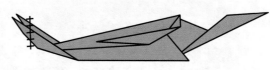

16

Completed part 2 of whale.

To Attach

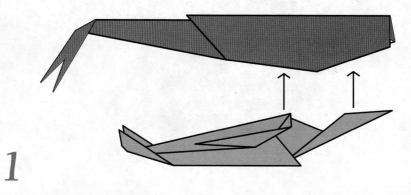

1

Position part 2 of whale into part 1. Glue to secure.

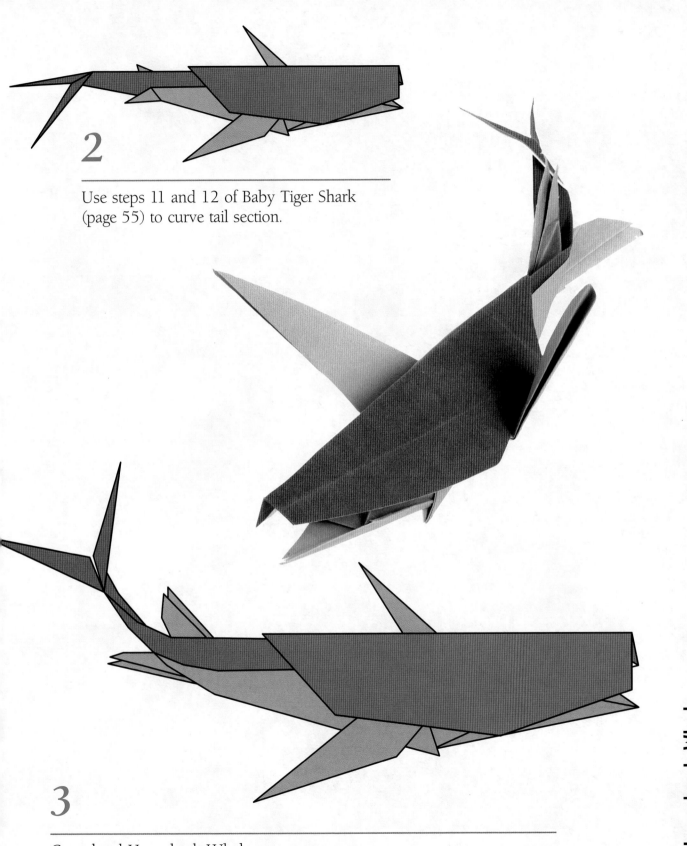

2

Use steps 11 and 12 of Baby Tiger Shark (page 55) to curve tail section.

3

Completed Humpback Whale.

Coral Fish

1

Valley fold in half.

2

Inside reverse folds.

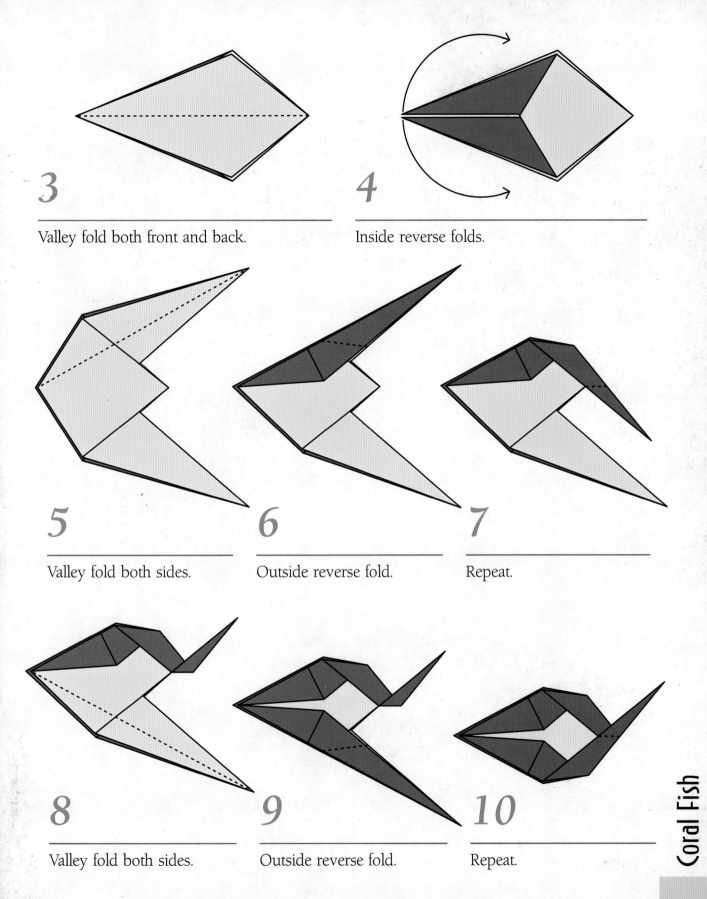

3

Valley fold both front and back.

4

Inside reverse folds.

5

Valley fold both sides.

6

Outside reverse fold.

7

Repeat.

8

Valley fold both sides.

9

Outside reverse fold.

10

Repeat.

Coral Fish

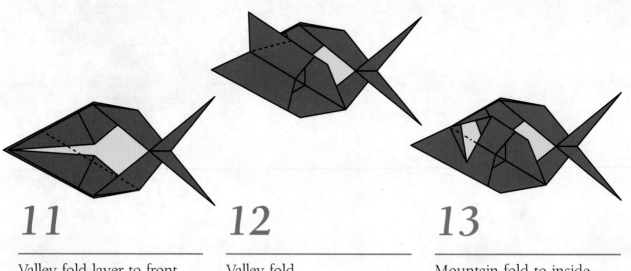

11
Valley fold layer to front.

12
Valley fold.

13
Mountain fold to inside.

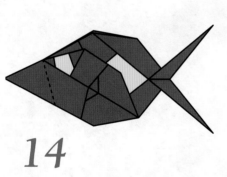

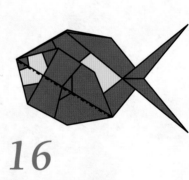

14
Valley fold.

15
Mountain fold to inside.

16
Mountain fold to back.

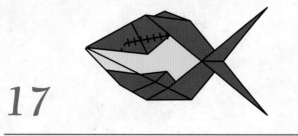

17
Cuts and valley out to sides both front and back.

Coral Fish

64

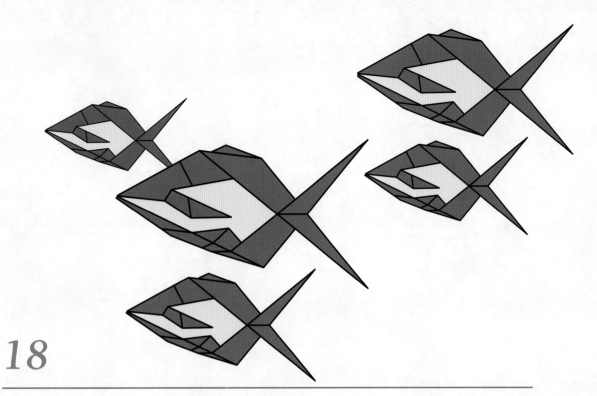

18

Completed Coral Fish

Swordfish

Part 1

1
Start with Base Fold III. Valley folds.

2
Turn over.

3
Cut front layers.

4
Valley folds.

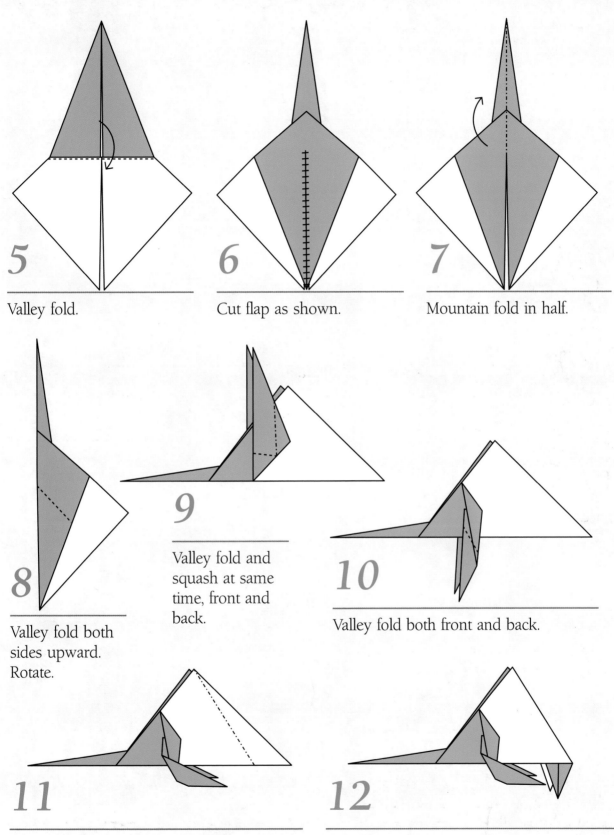

5

Valley fold.

6

Cut flap as shown.

7

Mountain fold in half.

8

Valley fold both sides upward. Rotate.

9

Valley fold and squash at same time, front and back.

10

Valley fold both front and back.

11

Mountain fold both front and back.

12

Completed part 1 of swordfish.

Swordfish

67

1

Cut paper (about 4" by 11") into diamond shape (see page 14). Turn over.

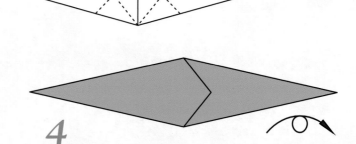

2

Complete folding into Base Fold IV.

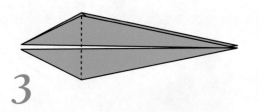

3

Valley fold.

4

Turn over.

5

Cuts to front layer.

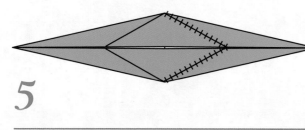

6

Valley open cut parts.

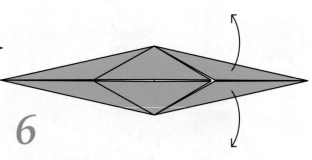

7

Cut as shown.

8

Valley fold.

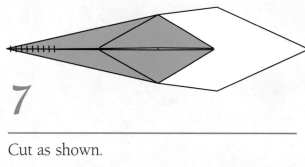

Swordfish

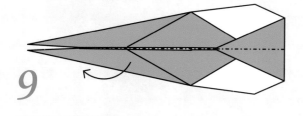

9

Mountain fold in half.

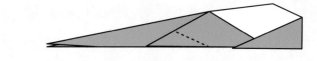

10

Valley fold both front and back.

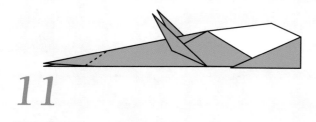

11

Valley fold both sides.

12

Completed part 2 of swordfish.

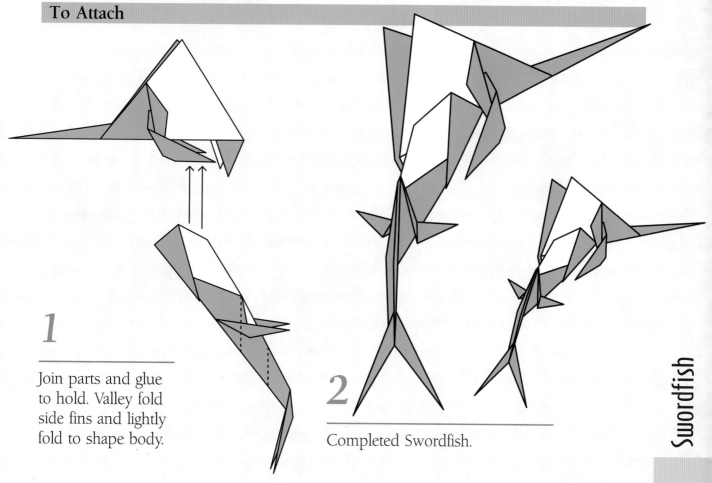

1

Join parts and glue to hold. Valley fold side fins and lightly fold to shape body.

2

Completed Swordfish.

King Crab

Part 1

1

Cut rectangular paper (about 4" by 11") into diamond shape (see page 14). Turn over.

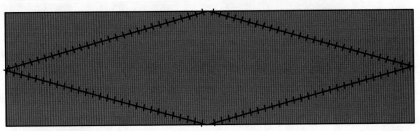

2

Continue folding into Base Fold IV.

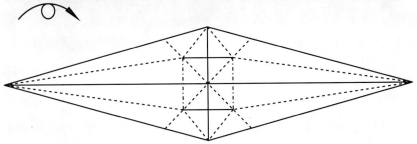

3

Valley fold both front and back.

4

Cut as shown on both sides.

5

Valley fold long flaps to right. Then valley first layer up and back layer down.

6

Valley fold.

7

Mountain fold.

8

Rotate.

9

Valley folds.

10

Mountain folds.

11

Inside reverse folds.

12

Make cuts as shown.

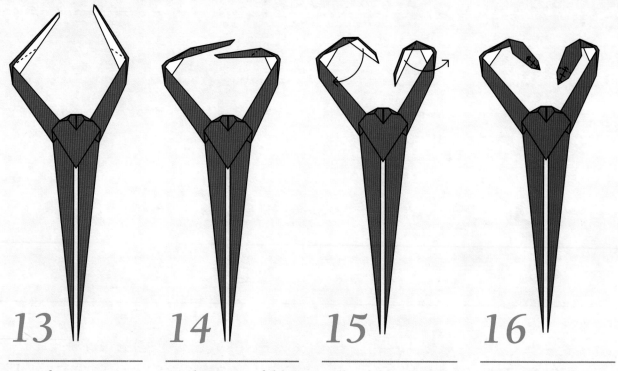

13

Outside reverse
folds.

14

Inside reverse folds.

15

Valley folds.

16

Cuts and loose
valley folds.

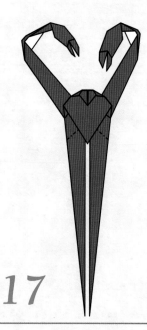

17

Mountain folds.

18

Valley folds.

19

Completed part 1 of crab.

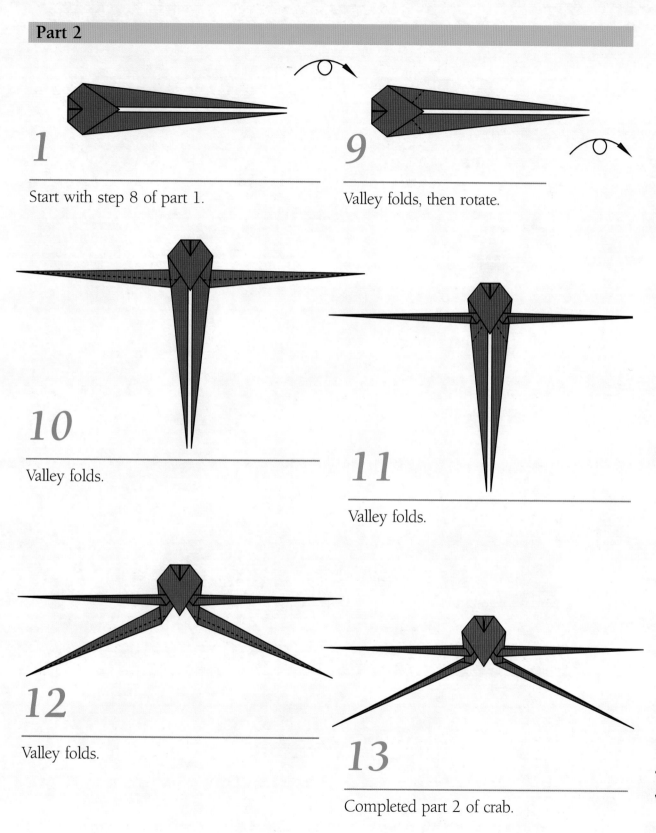

1

Start with step 8 of part 1.

9

Valley folds, then rotate.

10

Valley folds.

11

Valley folds.

12

Valley folds.

13

Completed part 2 of crab.

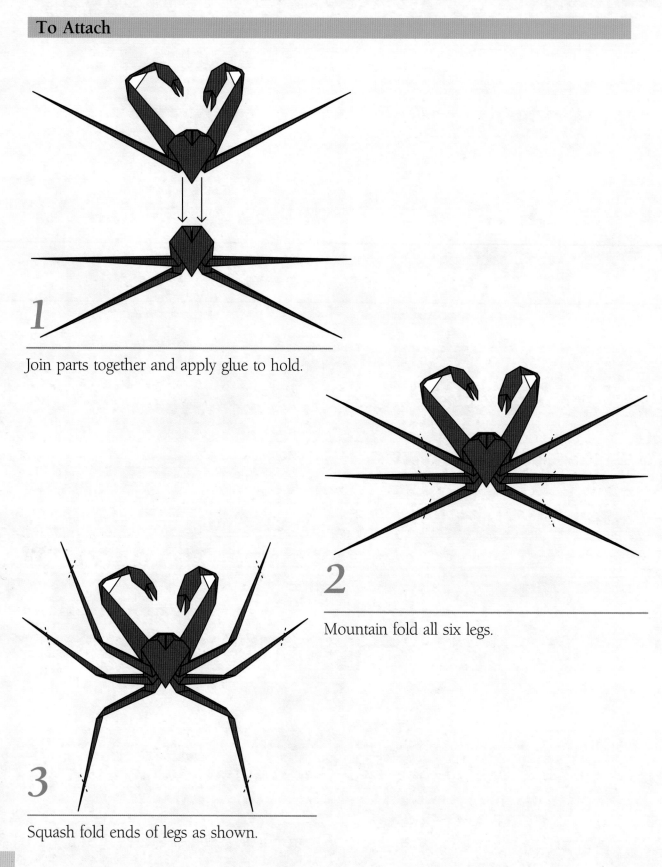

1

Join parts together and apply glue to hold.

2

Mountain fold all six legs.

3

Squash fold ends of legs as shown.

King Crab

74

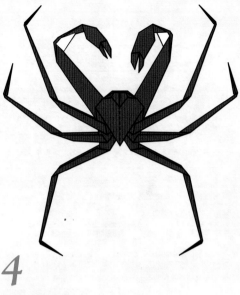

4

Mountain fold body in half,
then unfold to shape.

5

Completed King Crab.

Squid

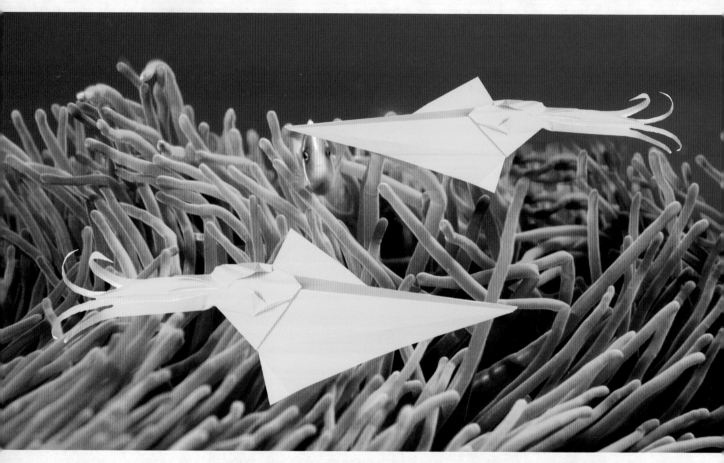

1

Start with rectangular paper (about 4" by 11"). Cut as shown (see page 14). Turn over.

2

Continue folding into Base Fold IV.

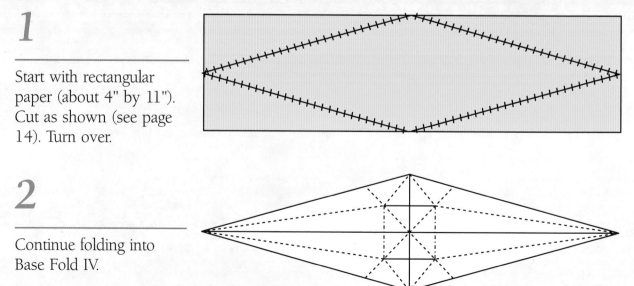

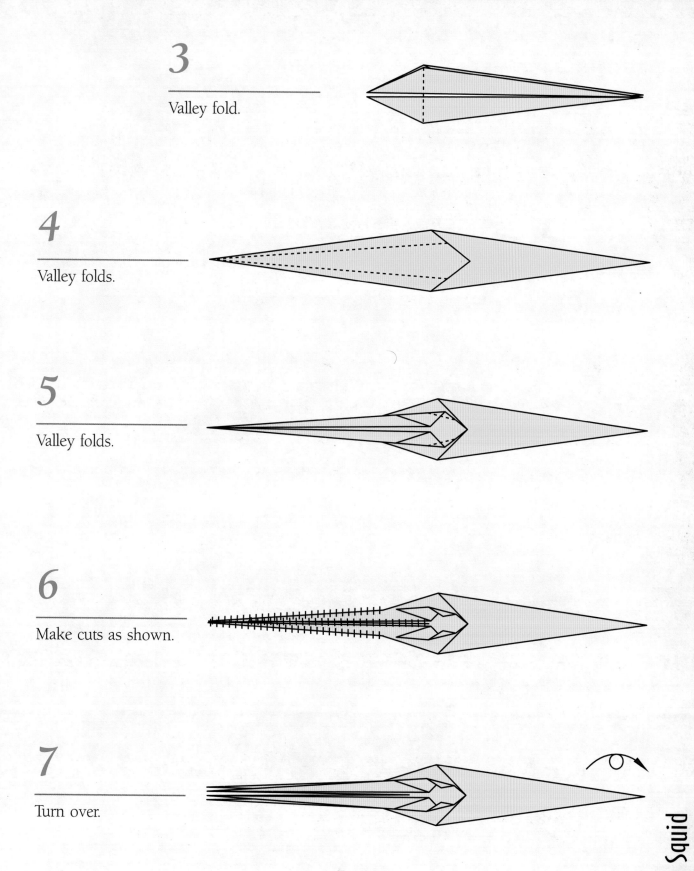

3

Valley fold.

4

Valley folds.

5

Valley folds.

6

Make cuts as shown.

7

Turn over.

Squid

8

Cuts to front layers.

9

Valley unfold cut parts.

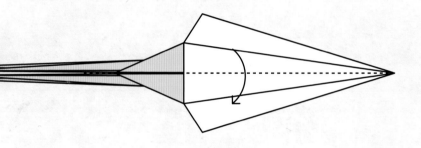

10

Valley fold in half.

11

Inside reverse fold.

12

Repeat inside reverse.

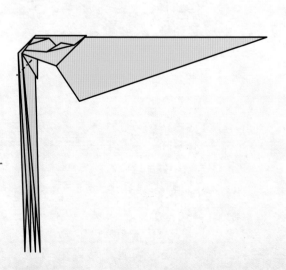

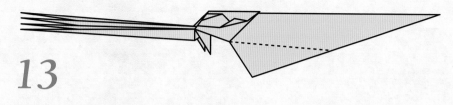

13

Valley fold both front and back.

14

Add curves to tentacles.

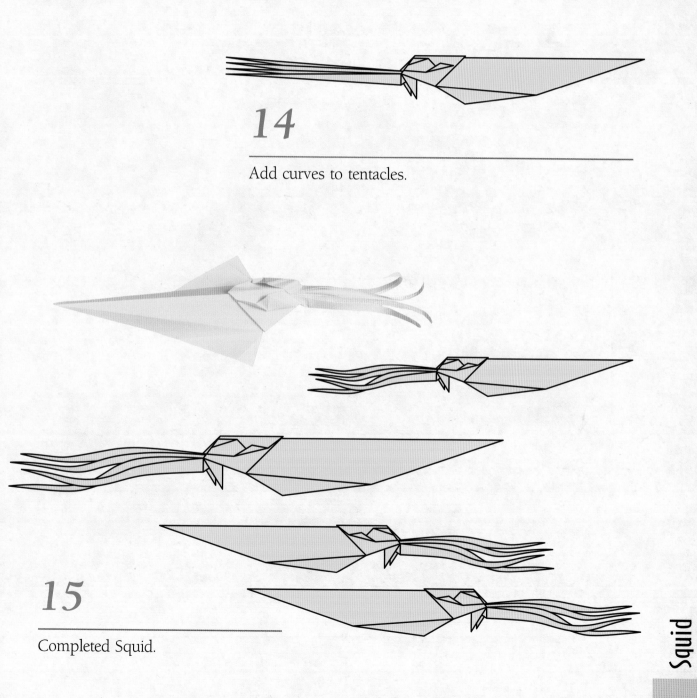

15

Completed Squid.

Blue Shark

Part 1

1

Cut rectangular paper (about 4" by 11") into diamond shape (see page 14). Turn over.

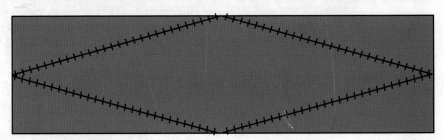

2

Continue folding into Base Fold IV.

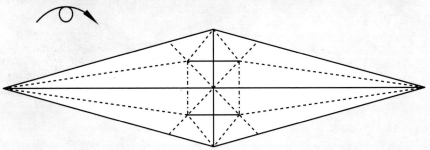

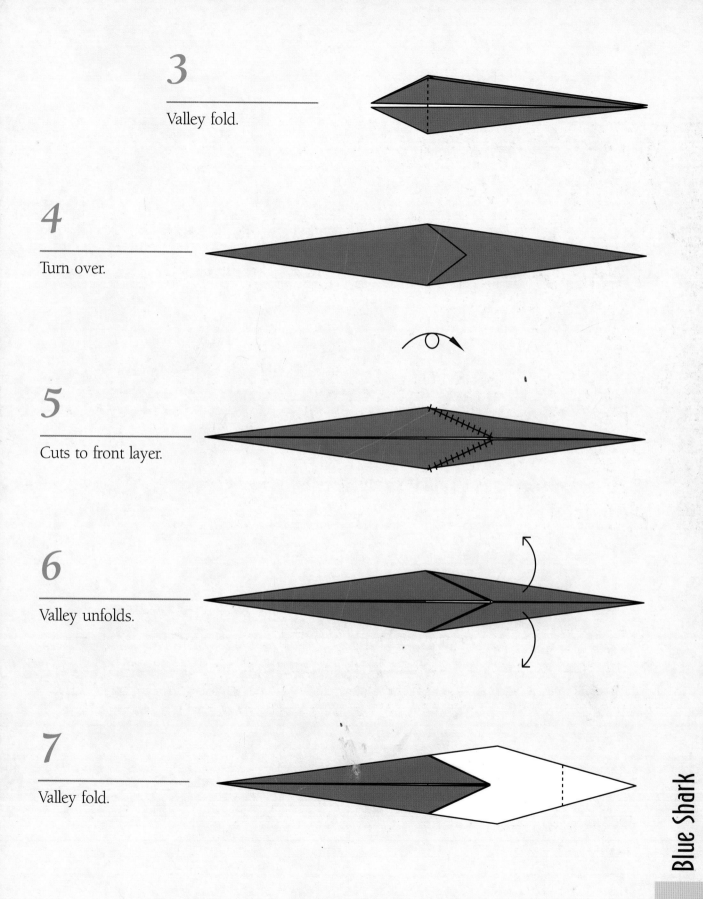

3

Valley fold.

4

Turn over.

5

Cuts to front layer.

6

Valley unfolds.

7

Valley fold.

Blue Shark

8

Valley folds.

9

Cuts as shown.

10

Valley folds, then
mountain fold in half.

11

Valley fold both sides.

12

Valley fold.

13

Completed part 1 of
shark.

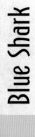

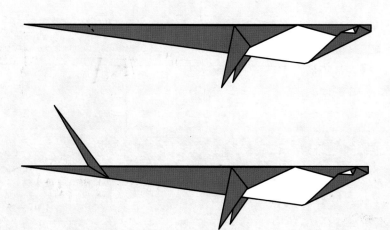

Blue Shark

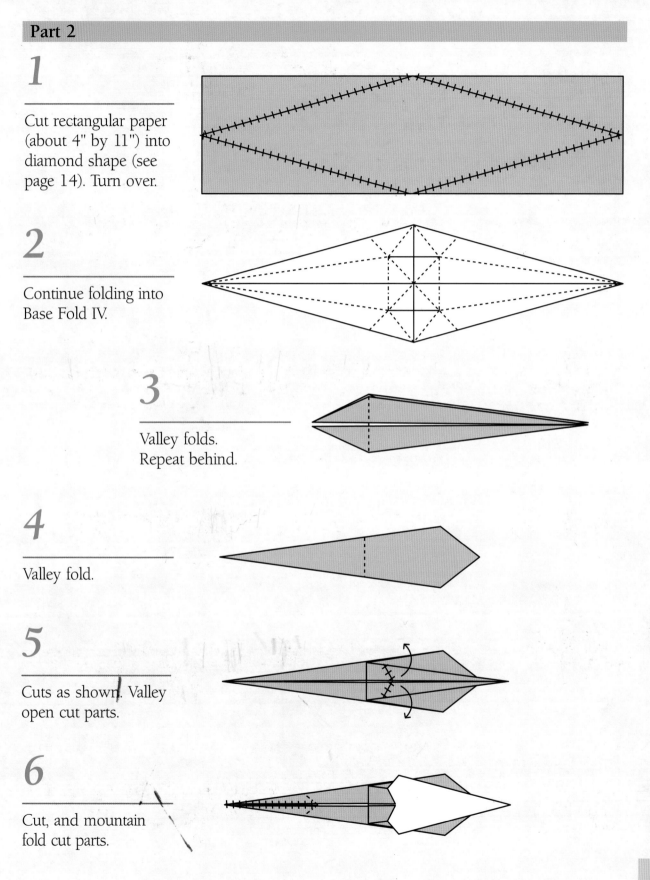

1

Cut rectangular paper (about 4" by 11") into diamond shape (see page 14). Turn over.

2

Continue folding into Base Fold IV.

3

Valley folds. Repeat behind.

4

Valley fold.

5

Cuts as shown. Valley open cut parts.

6

Cut, and mountain fold cut parts.

Blue Shark

7

Cut off ends as shown.

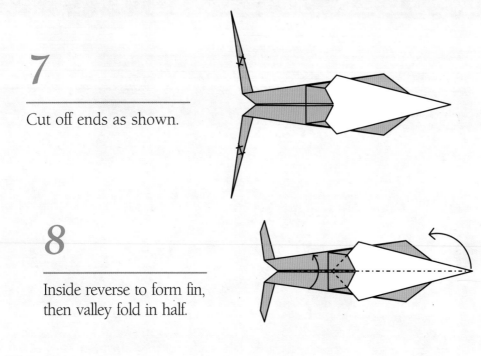

8

Inside reverse to form fin, then valley fold in half.

9

Mountain folds.

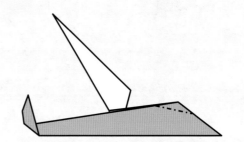

10

Cut as shown.

11

Completed part 2 of shark.

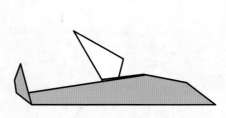

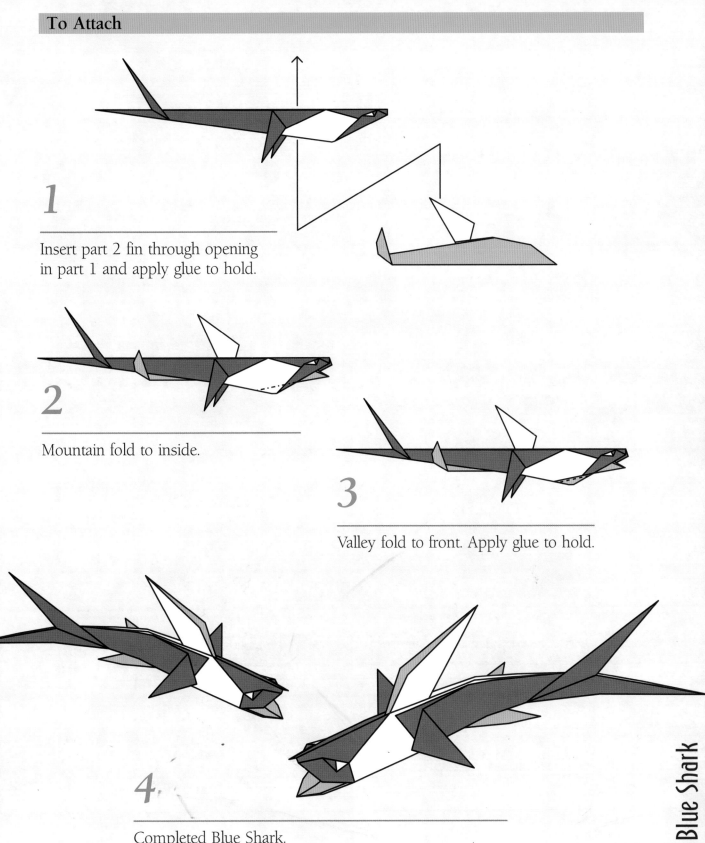

1

Insert part 2 fin through opening in part 1 and apply glue to hold.

2

Mountain fold to inside.

3

Valley fold to front. Apply glue to hold.

4

Completed Blue Shark.

Octopus

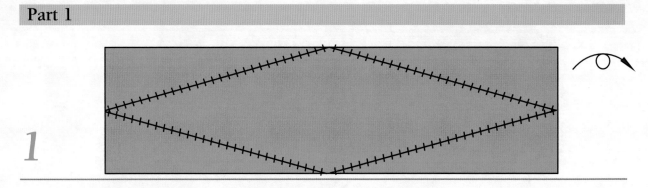

1

Cut rectangular paper (about 4" by 11") into diamond shape (see page 14). Turn over.

2

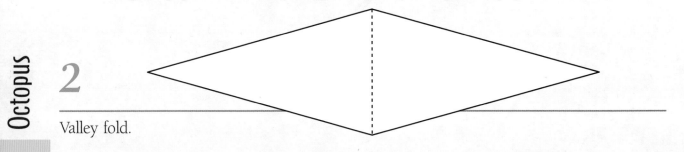

Valley fold.

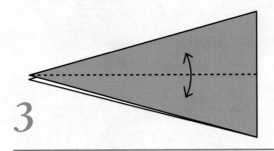

3

Valley fold and unfold.

4

Cut as shown.

5

Inside reverse folds.

6

Pull and valley fold along dashed line.

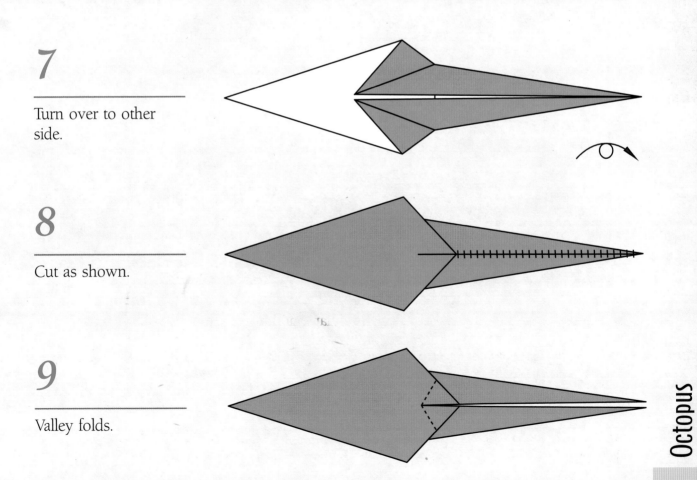

7

Turn over to other side.

8

Cut as shown.

9

Valley folds.

10

Squash folds.

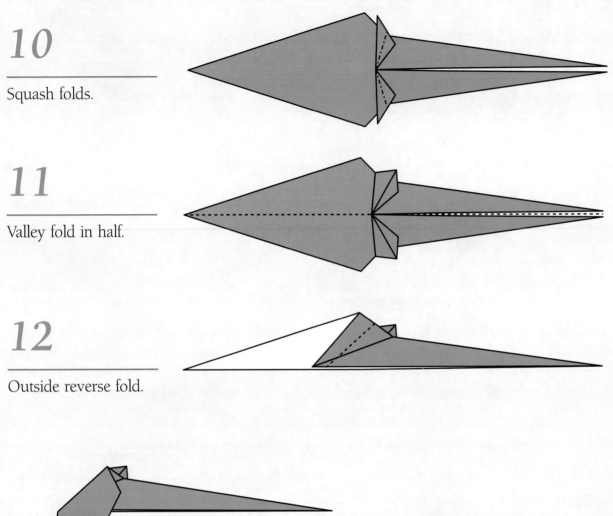

11

Valley fold in half.

12

Outside reverse fold.

13

Inside reverse fold.

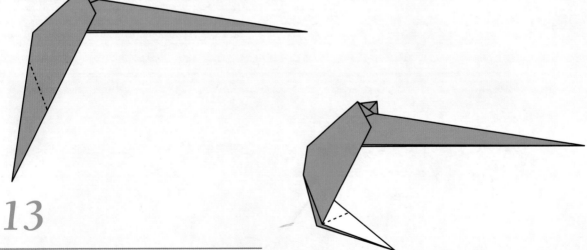

14

Outside reverse fold.

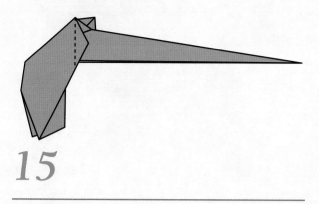

15

Valley fold both front and back.

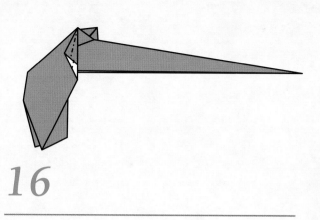

16

Squash fold both front and back.

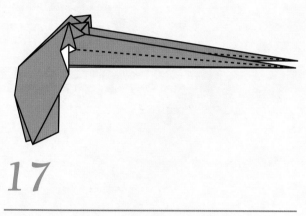

17

Valley fold both sides, and rotate.

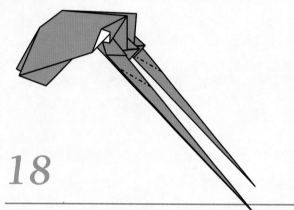

18

Mountain fold both front and back.

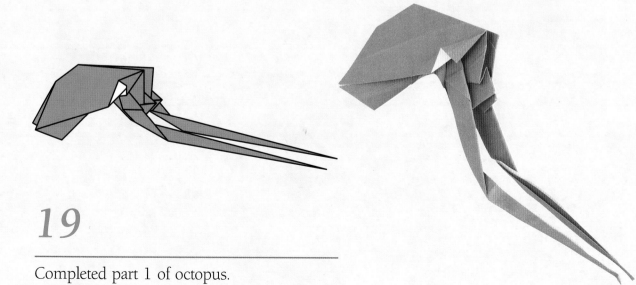

19

Completed part 1 of octopus.

Part 2

1

Base Fold IV.
Valley folds.

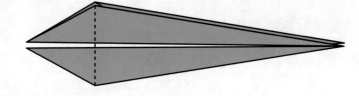

2

Valley fold both sides.

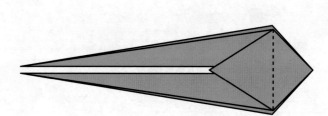

3

Valley fold both sides.

4

Valley folds again.

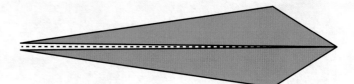

5

Cut both flaps and
return to last step.

6

Valley folds both sides.

7

Mountain fold in half.

8

Inside reverse fold.

9

Completed part 2
of octopus.

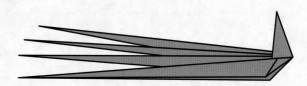

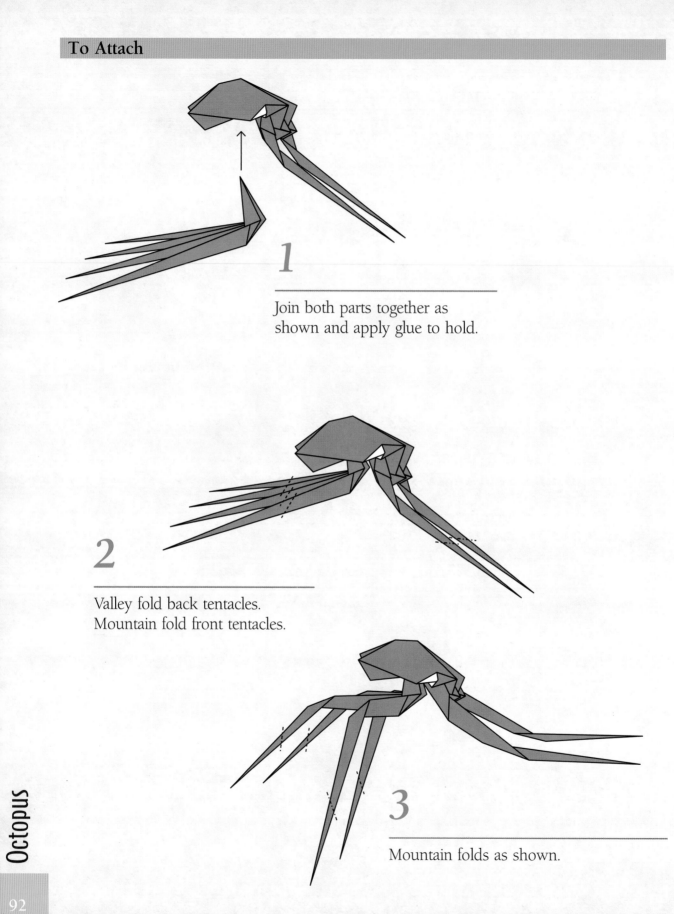

1

Join both parts together as
shown and apply glue to hold.

2

Valley fold back tentacles.
Mountain fold front tentacles.

3

Mountain folds as shown.

Octopus

92

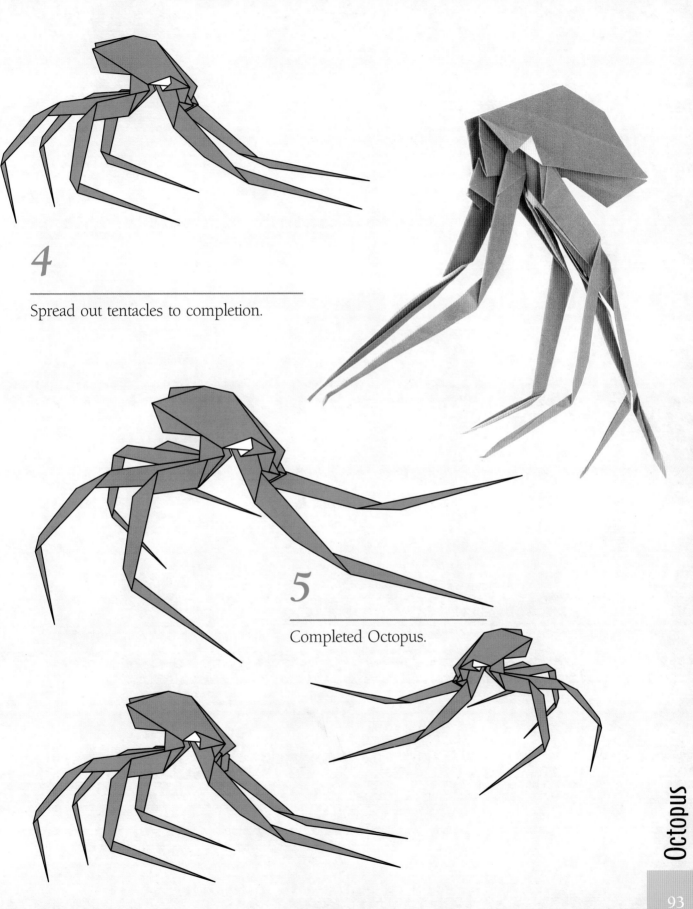

4

Spread out tentacles to completion.

5

Completed Octopus.

Stingray

Swordfish

Octopus

Coral
Fish

Dolphin

Seahorse

Under the Sea

Baby Tiger Shark

Humpback Whale

Lionfish

Barracuda

Electric Eel

Walrus

King Crab

Angelfish

Flying Fish

Hammerhead
Shark

Squid

Blue Shark

Horseshoe Crab

Index